JUNKIES,

HOOKERS,

DYKES...

...And Others I Have Known

Junkies, Hookers, Dykes
©2021 by Patricia Herd

This is a work of memoir, and while some names have been changed, the author has worked to be as accurate as possible. The people and places in this book are real, and the author apologizes for any error in their representation.

Published by Piscataqua Press
32 Daniel St., Portsmouth, NH 03801
www.ppressbooks.com

ISBN: 978-1-950381-74-6

Printed in the United States of America

JUNKIES,

HOOKERS,

DYKES...

...And Others I Have Known

Patricia Herd

To Puss...You Are My Sunshine

It was 1961. John Fitzgerald Kennedy had just been elected President. The Freedom Riders were working to integrate bus stations in the South. Vietnam was a long way from the horror it would become, and I ran off with my daughter's eighteen-year-old babysitter.

Up until that fateful event I was a straight, married, 27-year-old woman with an 18-month-old baby. Before marriage I had had many affairs with men, several of whom wanted to marry me. I had been a model in San Francisco, sold encyclopedias door to door, worked in a library, typed in a steno pool, was a switchboard operator and an aspiring actress. I had been around a block or two and had acquired several gay friends along the way, but never had the slightest interest in other women. So, running off with a young girl was pretty much out of my ken of knowledge, or as it turned out, my control.

Mindy lived in a house next door to our apartment with her sister and her sister's family. Mindy resembled an attractive teenage boy in her appearance and manner. Direct blue eyes, slender frame, clear skin devoid of makeup, blond hair braided loosely, jeans and boys' shirts. I had become friendly with her sister, and when the desert-tasting Santa Ana winds roared in I'd take my baby next door to let her play in the yellow plastic pool that was set up on their front lawn.

On occasion, Mindy would stop by on her way home from the junior college she was attending and say she would gladly baby-sit should we ever need help. My actor husband and I seldom went out as work was scarce, and he spent most of his time on the phone to his agent, looking for work or going on auditions. One day he got a call to audition for a play being sponsored by The Equity Library Theatre. He got the part and was thrilled to be in a company of good actors again and asked me if I would be okay with him being gone at night while he was rehearsing and then performing. I told him I thought it was a really terrific opportunity and the baby and I would be fine.

In reality, I wasn't fine. I wanted to be the one going to rehearsals, learning lines, being with the other actors. I really missed doing what I had wanted my whole life. Here we were in Hollywood, not New York where I had wanted to study. When two actors got married, at least in those days, one had to give up their dream, and in my experience, it was always the wife. So, I performed my duty, but the sacrifice led to discontent.

It was during those long nights between taking care of my child and ironing my husband's boxer shorts that Mindy started showing up just to hang out. She had similar interests to mine. We both enjoyed listening to music, in particular the guitarist Julian Breen and Joan Baez singing in that oh-so-haunting voice "The House of the Rising Sun." We talked about films we liked, and I told her my favorite movie of all time was *Gone With the Wind*, which Mother took me to see when I was four years old. Evidently, I sat there spellbound for the entire four hours and for every time I have seen it since. At night, when I had acted out my fantasies in front of the mirror in my bedroom in Ft. Worth, Texas, I was always Scarlett, the beautiful Southern Belle, the strong willed, tough, vain, manipulative woman-child who gave me the courage and the strength to survive my father's world of spirit-breaking beatings and despair. Nightly, I would escape into Scarlett's world of drama, tangled love affairs, intrigue, determination, hope, and survival.

Mindy, who had never seen the film — and was definitely not the type to fantasize — was sympathetic to my confession but had never experienced anything but love and acceptance in her young life. She was too young to understand the trauma that accompanies such a childhood as the one I had. I had experienced more in my 27 years than she could ever imagine. She had led a simple life and all she wanted was to be either a musician or an artist. With her there were no hidden agendas. She was who she was. No bullshit. No psychiatric help needed. I decided it best not to talk about my past life since she hadn't even been born for most of it and just to enjoy her company as it brought me some measure of escape from my life.

After a few weeks of hanging out, Mindy said, "I'm going to tell you something I have never told anyone." She took a deep breath. "I have never felt like I was a girl. I don't like 'girly' things. I always wanted to be a boy. On school days, my mom would stand by the front door to be sure I wasn't wearing my brother's clothes. Sometimes I would sneak something and change at school." She stopped and gave me a sideways glance, "I have feelings for women. I think I might be a lesbian." She seemed to expect a comment from me, but I had nothing to offer. She went on, "I think about being with a woman, but I have never done anything about it." She paused, "I have feelings for you. I want to be with you."

I carefully responded, "Well, Mindy, that's very flattering but you know I'm a lot older than you and I have a husband and a baby.

She said, "You and I have a lot in common and your age means absolutely nothing to me. I know you like me," she went on, "and I know you have feelings for me too." Yes, I liked her a lot, but I had never been with a woman before and while not repulsed by the idea, I was not the least bit interested.

AVALANCHE

After a week or so, while we were listening to Joni Mitchell and discussing whether or not Elizabeth Taylor should have won the Oscar for Butterfield Eight, I broached the elephant in the room.

"Mindy, I don't have any feelings for you other than liking you and there's no way I'm going to become involved with you so don't get your hopes up. You've just got a crush on me and someday you'll find someone more appropriate."

She said, "It's not a crush. I'm in love with you. I know you don't feel the same way, but could I at least just hug you?" A hug?

Oh my God. I had yearned for affection and love all my life, at first from my parents and then from my husband. When I hugged my mother, I was shooed away like a bothersome gnat. "Don't do that. You'll get me all wrinkled and sweaty."

My father had been loving when I was a baby, but later there were only whippings doled out instead of hugs. I had aunts and uncles who knew my situation at home and tried to make up for the lack of love, but it was never enough.

I heard myself saying to Mindy, "I would love to have a hug. That would be very nice." Well, that simple hug turned into me jumping off a cliff with no parachute. I was desperate for love, had been all my life, and here it was offered up like a lifeline for a drowning woman. The next thing I knew that hug turned into more, a lot more and soon we were making out like hungry dogs fighting over a piece of meat flung out the back door.

I found myself taking the baby to her sister's house, her sister gone for the day, putting the baby down for a nap and getting undressed. We stood naked in front of the full-length mirror in her room and just gazed at our images. She was young and perfect with a very slender body, small breasts and beautiful skin. I was taken aback when it felt so good to slide my hand along her smooth flank, and when she touched my breast, I moaned, "Oh my God, yes!" My senses reeled at her aroma of pure castile soap and the men's cologne she favored. Neither of us knew exactly how to go about getting down to business since she was a virgin and I had been taught that nice girls didn't do that sort of thing, but as our tongues and hands continued to explore this desire, the almost painful intensity and craving for one another was so great that, at twenty-seven years of age, I finally found out what all the excitement was about as I came and came and came. I was the other half of her, the top and the bottom of an Oreo cookie, the split of an atom.

It was amazing to suddenly experience something so powerful, enormous and greater than either of us. I felt like a boulder caught in an avalanche with the snow being a warm blanket and the ground as soft as a pillow.

After the amazing consummation of our affair, we continued to meet on the sly as often as we could and making love just got better and better, growing deeper and stronger. When

I was with her, the air smelled sweeter and everything around me glowed. I glowed. Even my husband, who never complimented me in any way, said I looked better. Better than what? I thought. I must have really looked like shit. One time when we were dressed up to go out, I asked him if he thought I was pretty. He took a good look at me and replied, "No, not pretty. I'd have to say that you're a handsome woman." I just stood there trying to absorb "handsome." Why the fuck couldn't he just lie for once? Anyway, I no longer needed his approval. I was beautiful in Mindy's eyes.

1963

PANDORA'S BOX

I began actively planning a way to actually be with Mindy. I decided that if I got some kind of job at night when the baby was asleep, maybe I could earn enough for us to run away together. Theo was through with the play and would be able to be home with the baby while I was working. I had to broach the idea carefully lest he get suspicious. One day after putting the baby down for a nap, I came into our living room and sat down on our faux Danish sofa.

"I think it would be a good idea for me to find a night job since you're not working," I began. He was pacing up and down the length of the room, still in his robe at 2:00 in the afternoon. It had been one of those horrible dry periods all actors suffer through until the next job. He was not in a good mood. I continued my lie.

"We need the extra money and maybe you would feel better without so much pressure on you," I said. There was no use suggesting that he get some kind of temporary job just to "help out" unless I wanted to listen to a litany of how demeaning it would be for an ACTOR of his talent and genius to actually work at a day job. Theo continued pacing.

"God damn it," he loudly protested. "The Goddamn agent isn't doing shit. I am an ACTOR," he said, raising his voice. "I'm just wasting my talent out here in this God forsaken hell hole!" He stopped pacing and looked at me. After a long pause he said, "I guess that might be a good idea."

We worked it out that Theo would stay home with the baby and work on Shakespeare or Ibsen or some such while I brought home the bacon. That it was to be my bacon, not ours, was beside the point.

I had absolutely no qualms about lying to the man who, despite his anger and insecurity, was in love with me and cared deeply about my welfare. He was a wonderful father to our daughter and tried to be a good husband. That my choice to run away with Mindy would cause terrible pain, dismay and upheaval never entered my mind, or if it did, I was so besotted and determined that I didn't care.

Near our apartment, I had seen a coffee/jazz club called Pandora's Box. At that time there was a small strip of land occupied by this club right in the middle of Crescent Heights where Laurel Canyon crossed over Sunset. Schwab's Drugstore was on Sunset to the east of The Box where mostly out of work actors hung out by the bank of telephone booths that lined the back wall, waiting for the magical call that would change their lives. Supposedly, Lana Turner was discovered sipping a soda at Schwab's. On the west side of Crescent was a bank and a strip mall where once had been the sprawling apartment hotel called The Garden of Allah. The Garden was built as a private residence in 1917 for Alla Nazimova, the openly lesbian silent movie star who was infamous for her wild and debauched parties. In 1927, she erected an exotic complex of 25 villa/apartments that were occupied by famous movie stars and literary figures such as F. Scott Fitzgerald, Hemingway and Greta Garbo. After The Garden's heyday had passed, assorted characters and denizens of the night lived and hung out there until it was torn down in 1959.

I decided that since The Box was close to where we lived, I would first try to get a job there. The next afternoon I dressed in my most provocative outfit: tight jeans and a peasant blouse that I let slide slightly off the shoulders. I walked down the street and and into what I imagined the inside of a brothel in Istanbul would look like. The manager came over and looked me up and down.

"Yeah, what can I do for you kid?"

I lied and said I had a lot of experience waitressing in San Francisco at a coffee house there. They must have been pretty desperate because the manager said, "Sure, kid, start tonight at 8."

I was stunned. I ran home with my good news only to find my husband still ranting.

"I can't deal with this shit anymore," he said. I tried to calm him down, but the intensity of his anger grew until he was yelling at full force, which was really overwhelming.

"Stop, listen to me," I screamed uselessly. There was never a way to override those rages. He finally calmed down enough for me to tell him of my good fortune.

He grudgingly said, "What time do you get off?

"Two," I said.

"OK, be careful coming home."

After a thankfully quiet dinner I went to my new job. You couldn't miss The Box. It was painted purple and orange and where the paint wasn't peeling had a sort of jazzy vibe to it. There was a back entrance that the help was supposed to use and as I entered the cool vibe turned to cacophony. "Gimmie two on the side," yelled one waitress picking up an order. "I said espresso, not regular!" screamed another. I don't think I can do this, I thought as a woman named Sandra came over.

"You must be the new victim," she said. "Come on, I'll get you started." She was a Godsend. She showed me the menu and what all the coffee orders meant. Hot, cold, espresso, latte, cappuccino, regular and a selection of pastries. I quickly tried to memorize some of the most popular drinks, but Sandra told me not to worry because, "Things are pretty loose around here."

In the main smoked-filled room, there was a large psyche-delic mural and a small stage where the talent performed. Most of the patrons were adults, but teens were welcome also since no liquor was served. However, in my short time working at The Box, I saw many a bottle of booze passed around seemingly unnoticed by the management and drugs were discretely dispensed in the grimy bathroom. I was able to hold my own as most of the crowd were pretty laid back and were forgiving with my fumbled orders. I was interested in the jazz as it reminded me of my time in the San Francisco jazz clubs. One of my favorites, Les McCann, was a regular, and other would-be jazz musicians or budding rock stars performed there.

There were plenty of characters in and out of The Box. One of the waitresses in particular piqued my interest. I never knew her name, as she was as reclusive as she was strange. I couldn't tell whether or not she was pretty since her long, dirty blond hair completely covered one side of her face. She either had a physical condition or she had seen the Gloria Graham film, *The Big Heat* where Lee Marvin throws scalding coffee on Gloria's face, disfiguring her for life. Her famous line was, "I can always go through life sideways." And that is exactly what this gal did. She never turned that side of her face toward you. When talking an order, she would swivel like an eel toward the direction of the customer, stringy hair hanging over the small table and then slip slide away toward the kitchen. I thought maybe it was a gimmick that some of the girls used to increase their tips until one day I was out with the baby in the stroller and I saw her walking down the street "going through life sideways."

I lasted at The Box for several months, and that was certainly longer than some of the other jobs I had held. It was interesting from a sociological point of view, but my waitressing skills were poor at best and the tips I counted out every night when I got home were not enough to help out or to escape.

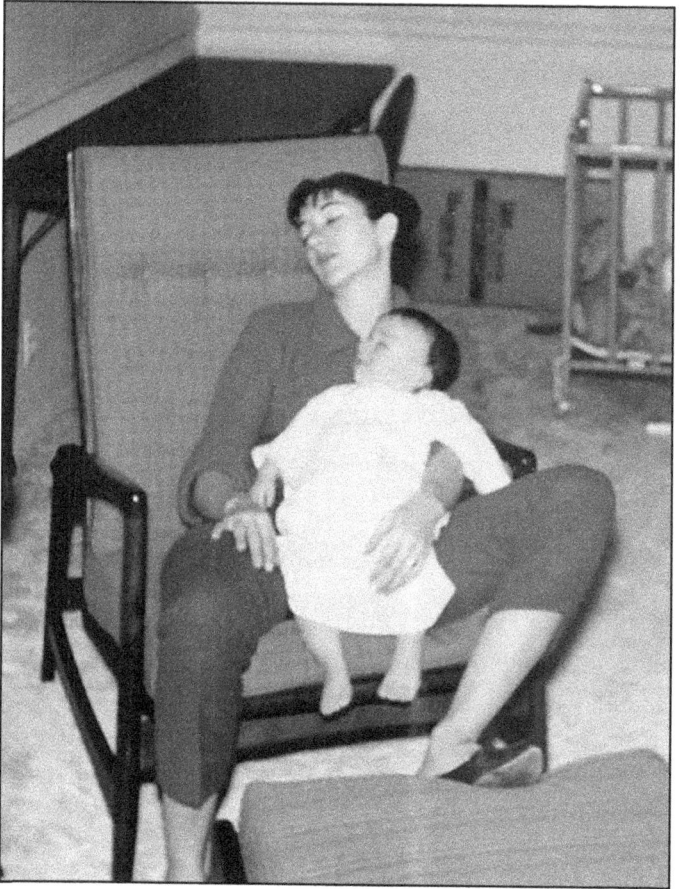

MANHATTAN BEACH
1962

I finally got enough courage to tell Theo that I needed some time away to think about our marriage, which, as both of us knew, was faltering. Taking Mindy along to care for the baby while I looked for a job was not questioned.

I had always liked the beach towns south of L.A.: Hermosa Beach, Redondo Beach and Manhattan Beach. These towns were quaint and old fashioned in those days, laid back and quiet. Almost every day I drove down Lincoln Boulevard and onto the Pacific Coast Highway to try to find a cheap rental where I could start my life over. In one such foray I found a beautiful old two-story house in Manhattan Beach that was partly furnished. It had a living room, dining room, kitchen and bath on the ground floor and on the second floor a small bedroom with an alcove that was perfect for the baby. The house was musty, old and moldy but it would do. With help from Mindy's sister and my husband, we moved in a few pieces of furniture: the baby's crib, a dresser and a piece or two that Mindy's sister gave her. There was a bed upstairs and I bought a new mattress. By this time, my husband had gotten a job or two playing "hoods" on TV and said he would pay the rent until I could find work.

Mindy and I were in the "honeymoon" stage of our affair and it was the happiest time of my life up to that time. We spent hours and days painting the old kitchen, trying to cover the decades of grease and grime on the walls. There was an old O'Keefe and Merritt stove that no matter how much we scrubbed refused to give up its grime. It had two ovens that still worked and two burners out of four were usable. There were pots and pans that had seen better days, glassware, mismatched utensils for four, and other assorted kitchenware that had just been left by previous tenants and not removed by the old couple who owned the house. With the downside came surprises as in one of the junk-filled closets I actually found a working sewing machine and was able to make some kitchen curtains. The owners didn't seem to care what we did with the house, so we hauled off the shit-stained shag rug that covered the bedroom floor and finally got some shine back on the once-beautiful wood floors. We worked, scrubbed, shined and hauled. Everything we did was new and exciting and fun. In my memory it was a magical time, and we were so fully and deeply in love that there was nothing else but our joy in just being together.

Unfortunately, you can't live on love, so I had to get a job. I had learned how to operate a switchboard when I lived in New York, before my husband and I married, and found a job as an operator at a hospital in Hermosa Beach. The hours were good, and the pay was enough for the rent and food. My husband had agreed to send a little something for the baby, so we were able to get by.

On weekends when I was off work we would go to the beach for picnics. We built sandcastles, ate cheese sandwiches and watched the baby happily nattering away. That the castles were only made of sand, built and then washed away never entered my mind until later.

One day while basking in the sunlight, Mindy said, "Wouldn't it be great if we could have a baby?" I was shocked. It would be many decades before lesbians could marry and have children.

I said, "Mindy, that's absolute nonsense. Who's going to be the mother of this imaginary baby? Not me, that's for sure and I really can't see you getting pregnant. And, of course, there's the question of a father."

Mindy said, "Well, I thought it would be nice." Nice! I was always surprised when she acted like a teenager. I had fooled myself into thinking that we were the same age, with the same experiences but she was just a kid and I was making assumptions based on nothing but my own desires.

Sometimes Mindy's brother would come to visit. He was also gay but hadn't come out yet. He was a very sweet and dear boy. Younger than Mindy by two years, he was very feminine and beautiful with his big blue eyes and blond curls hanging over his chiseled forehead. It was as though, even with the two-year difference in their ages, they had somehow gotten mixed up in the womb.

Friends, from what I now called my old life, wanted to visit but I was terrified of anyone knowing what was going on. To be homosexual and especially a lesbian in those days was very hidden and underground. I had a child, and I could not take any chances that she would be taken away from me. Since I didn't know who or what I was, the very idea of being judged and labeled by others was terrifying.

I had not even confided in my best friend Harriett, who wanted to come down and bring her baby, but I told her I needed to be alone and couldn't see her. She was confused and angry but continued to call until finally she stopped.

Many years later when I tried to renew our friendship, Harriett said, "You know Pat, if you had told me what was going on, I never would have stopped being your friend. I understand that these things happen, but now I'm just not interested in picking up where we left off. Too much time has passed, and I've moved on." Of course, she was right.

My friend Jim from my old Alley Theatre days in Houston found out where we were living and came for a visit. "What are you doing? What's going on?" he asked.

"I'm just really mixed-up, Jim, and I can't talk about it." I wanted to cry on his shoulder and relieve myself of this terrible burden but was too afraid.

I was basically alone with two children: my baby and my lover who was not old enough or wise enough to understand the strain and attendant pain that I constantly endured.

TRAUMA

In the midst of my swinging wildly between euphoria and agony, a diary Mindy kept and in which she graphically described our relationship and our sex lives in flowery detail was found by my husband and read on one of his visits to see our daughter. He had begun to suspect that Mindy was more than just a babysitter, and in a fit of rage called my parents, who flew in from Texas and threatened to take the baby away unless I left Mindy immediately. It was a scene out of a Tennessee Williams play. Mother pulling on one tiny arm of the child and me on the other, screaming at one another until the poor little waif began convulsing which stopped the whole thing cold.

"That's enough, Mom," I screamed. "I promise not to see Mindy anymore. Just let go of the baby!"

The woman who had never loved me let go of my baby and said, "It's against the law what you're doing. We didn't raise you to be a queer!"

I sat down on the stairs, baby in arms, and just sobbed. "Please, please don't take her. I'll do anything you want, only please don't take my baby!"

My father, who had been strangely quiet during all this terrible drama said, "We're not going to take her, but you straighten up, you hear?"

I cried holding on tight to my precious child. "Yes, yes, I

promise."

When my parents showed up Mindy had split, but the day after my parents left, she came to the house. I couldn't talk to her.

She said, "Why are you sending me away? They're gone. Why can't I come back?"

I said, "Mindy, the laws are very stringent about homosexuality and you don't seem to understand that my parents could take away my child if we stay together."

She protested, "I'll always love you and I know you love me. Nothing will happen. They're just mad, but they'll get over it."

I could barely contain my rage, "It's the law, God damnit, Mindy! It's against the fucking law what we're doing in the eyes of most people. Can't you get that through your head?" Mindy didn't answer. She picked up her things saying she would be at her sister's waiting for me to call.

I was facing a real threat and no matter how much I cared for Mindy I couldn't take the chance of losing my child. She was the one person in my life who loved me unconditionally and depended on me to take care of her and to love her. I made up my mind that I had to be responsible and vowed to always be there for my daughter, and that, no matter what was going on in my life, she would come first. Many times, in our lives together, I have failed to keep that promise to her, but I have tried to do the best I can, and she has and always will come first.

Theo wanted us to come home, but I just couldn't go back, not now. I returned to L.A., got a furnished apartment and found a job in an insurance office, typing. There was a good daycare center near the apartment, and we agreed that Theo would take care of our daughter every other weekend.

I tried not to think of Mindy, but the sexual need was just too strong. I had to see her, to be with her. We started seeing one another whenever we could without my husband finding out. It was a nightmare for both of us, and she particularly resented having to hide our relationship. The age difference became an issue with me, coupled with the impossibility of going to a nice restaurant or even the movies as she absolutely refused to make any attempt to look straight. "Why can't you just put on a little lipstick and fix your hair?" I complained. "I feel extremely uncomfortable when people stare at us."

Mindy didn't care. "I know who I am," she said. "It's OK when we're alone, but you seem to be embarrassed by me when we go out. I'm sorry that you aren't able to see me for who I am and accept it. I don't need 'fixing up.' I'm just fine the way I am. You need to figure out who you really are."

I felt terrible. She was right, but I just couldn't admit it. I was afraid of what people might think when seeing us out together. What they might infer. I was also deeply conflicted about my feelings for Mindy. Was I in love with her or was it strictly sexual? Was I using her as an excuse to leave my husband, although I found myself missing him on an intellectual level and the connection we had with the theatre. The only real connection I had with Mindy, outside of the bedroom, was a common interest in music and movies. I was beginning to think that maybe that wasn't enough.

VEGAS
1963

During this time of pain and confusion on my part, Theo was offered a job in Las Vegas to play the villain in a melodrama, The Drunkard at the New Frontier Hotel, one of the original hotels before the strip became "The Strip." As one last attempt to get back together, he asked if I would come with him to Vegas as part of the company. Theo had talked to the producer saying that his wife was an actress and as there were several roles for which I was right the producer agreed. He also added that we each would get $500 a week, which certainly cinched the deal for me as that was more money than I had seen in a long time.

I called Mindy and said, "I'm going to Vegas with Theo to do a show. I am confused and the only thing I do know for sure is that I really miss you, but I feel trapped." I didn't even know what I meant by "trapped" except maybe trapped in my own mind by the assumption that other people's views, opinions and standards were valid. "I'm hoping that this time away will clarify things for me."

Mindy said, "I don't understand what's going on with you. It's simple. I love you. You love me. What more clarification do you need?"

I took a six-week leave of absence from my job, got an actor friend to sublet my apartment and called my parents to ask if they would take care of the baby while we were working. They were thrilled, not only to have time with their grandchild, but also because they hoped that their son-in-law and I would reunite. Strange coming from people who wouldn't even come to our wedding, but since the arrival of the baby the ice had begun to melt, and they became loving grandparents. I was amazed to see a different side of both of them as they cooed and awed over the baby and began sending gifts and money. I didn't question this reversal but really enjoyed being with them and accepted the love I had always yearned for.

In Vegas, Theo and I arrived at the hotel and walked into a time warp. The Last Frontier Hotel/Casino had been one of the first hotels on the strip, and by an amazing coincidence was the same hotel where my parents and I stayed on a road trip from Texas in 1947. In my memory the hotel hadn't changed at all. Even though it had been refurbished and the name had been changed to The New Frontier, it was the same old early Vegas joint. The entertainment was even the same. The "Original" Ink Spots were playing, and, with an addition or two, I believe they were the same group I had thrilled to sixteen years earlier.

We were shown the small space where we were to perform, met the rest of the cast and were shown our roach-infested dressing rooms. It certainly was not the glitzy glamour of Vegas I had been expecting and on top of that we had to do three shows a night starting at ten with only one day off. We were going to really have to work for our money.

We rented a small apartment near the theatre and started

rehearsing. This was before any legit shows had been done in Vegas and the producer had high hopes that we would be a big hit. The cast, by and large, was very good. I played a Salvation Army missionary and also another small part, so I was kept pretty busy just changing clothes and makeup three times a night.

When the last show was over at 4:00 AM, we all went across the street to the Desert Inn, more commonly known as the DI, to have breakfast and to wind down a bit. We became friendly with a cute little guy who was the night pit boss, "Peanuts." He had an eye for "the girls" and we teased him and had fun playing up to him. He in turn got us tickets for all the best shows happening in Vegas then. We saw Sinatra, up close and personal, Judy Garland and other top entertainers of that era. One night before the show, Peanuts took us to an Italian place in downtown Vegas. There were a lot of large Italian men and big haired, bejeweled women who all seemed to know Peanuts and stopped by our table to show their respect while their women smiled beguilingly. We were curious but didn't think much about it as we were having such a good time with our new friend until we got back to LA, and read a book called *The Green Felt Jungle* in which we discovered that Peanuts was a nickname for a well-connected Mafia capo. So much for my ability to judge people.

We finally opened to very small houses. Turned out that people would rather gamble than sit for two hours to watch a melodrama more mellow than drama, so our producer's dream of greatness was not to be realized.

During this time in Vegas, Theo and I tried sex several

times. To his credit, he really tried to give me what he thought I needed, but his fumbled attempts at cunnilingus just made me miss Mindy more. One night after the show I called her, said I needed to be with her and sent her a ticket to Vegas. I didn't think of the impact it would have on my husband to have my lover show up out of the blue. I also didn't stop to think how it would affect Mindy. My dread of being labeled came true, since as soon as she came backstage after the show, the nature of our relationship was obvious. While most of the cast members withheld any judgement, there was one, a real jerk, who started making snide remarks. "I smell a dyke in here. We better get the dyke spray!" Soon, some of the others joined in on the fun. It was a disaster for Mindy, who took the first plane back to LA. It was a huge embarrassment for my husband, and a really shitty thing to have done to him. In short, it was an all-around major fuck-up. When it finally dawned on me what I had done, I felt horrible, but by then it was too late.

Since Mindy had never encountered what gays and lesbians routinely endured and had never understood why I had been, up until this debacle, so secretive, it must have been devastating to have been thrown to the wolves by the person she most loved and trusted. It took a long time to gain that trust back only to have it eroded time and time again by me until there was no trust or love left.

Three weeks into the run, my parents called to say they were just not up to taking care of an active toddler full time. Dad and grandchild flew in, the baby was handed over, and Dad got back on the plane and left. While we certainly understood their decision, it put a terrible burden on an already impossible situation. My husband and I were struggling just to do three shows a night and try to maintain some semblance of sanity and politeness after the Mindy debacle. Neither of us wanted to talk about what had happened, but I sensed that he finally saw it as the end to whatever relationship he had hoped for.

We developed a method where one of us would stay up when we got home from the show at 6:00 AM to take care of our daughter while the other slept until noon when we changed places. The babysitter we had hired came at 7:00 so we would have some time for dinner before going to the theatre. It was a bitch and really increased an already tense situation. The name-calling persisted from the asshole and several others. I felt as though I was on a Ferris wheel from Hell. It never stopped and I couldn't get off. Those three weeks were endless and unrelenting, but we both did the best we could in trying to be good parents and in trying to be at least civil to one another in front of our child. We finally finished the show, collected our money, flew home and Theo went one way and baby and I the other. The one thing I did learn from this experience was that words could not harm me, or my child. No one threatened me, no one called Child Services… they were simply words.

The first thing I did when the baby and I got to our apartment was to call Mindy. She sounded cool and aloof. "I really don't think I can go through this anymore," she said. "You treat me like shit, like some old shoe. It's just too much. I don't want to be with you anymore."

"I know, I know…you're right," I said, "I promise that things will be different if you will just come back. I will be totally committed. We could start over. I miss you so much. I'll tell my husband that I really want to be with you and that's the way it's going to be!" She reluctantly agreed.

When she walked in the door, I realized I couldn't live without her. I didn't care if she dressed like Tonto or his horse Scout. She just looked so beautiful to me. She was the missing tooth that a kid probes and probes with his tongue until the new one grows in. We spent the night pretzeled together, spent and exhausted by the magic of being one. I felt right about our relationship for the first time, all the questions put on hold and I decided to enjoy whatever I might be labeled. I stopped caring about others and my own doubts for a lovely period of time. I even talked to my husband and he finally realized that we were never going to mend our broken lives and agreed to a divorce. There was nothing to divide and since he already paid a small amount of child support, we had no reason to go to court. I went downtown to the courthouse, filled out some papers, got them notarized and it was a done deal. Divorce granted.

When I called my parents to tell them that Theo and I had finally called it quits, Mom asked me if I had gone back with that queer. I lied through my teeth, but it was obvious she knew, since she ended the conversation by saying, "I know you're lying, but as long as you take care of my grandbaby properly, I'm not going to say or do anything." I put the phone down and just stood looking at it. After two long years of constant fear and worry, I would finally be able to live my life free of the vision of the two of them swooping down like avenging carrions taking my precious little girl with them.

ENCINO

1963-1964

The next day I went out looking for a place and found a charming cottage behind a church in Encino on a narrow lane with only a few houses. It was California ranch style and was ready to move in. No more scrubbing and hauling and no mold! It was unfurnished, but the rent was reasonable and between the two of us, some thrift stores and my ex's monthly contribution for our daughter's care we managed. I cooked on an outdoor barbeque until I could afford to buy a 1927 yellow and black stove. I really loved that stove, and it became the center of my kitchen life.

The house had two bedrooms, nice wood floors, a dining area, den and a living room with a fireplace. It was charming and Mindy put her creative touches everywhere to make it homey. She would find a fir cone and arrange it with a flower so that it looked like a work of art. Everything she touched lent beauty to our home. She made beautiful hand-bound books about a little girl just like my daughter. They were beautifully illustrated in watercolor and were all about a little girl's life and adventures. My daughter loved those books and wanted them read to her over and over until she had them memorized.

Mindy was the most loving mother that the little girl had. She was patient, not one of my virtues, firm without judgment. And the child, who certainly needed stability, blossomed without the drama that had been part of her life for too long. We bought a swing set and rescued a yellow kitten that endured too much love from a happy little girl.

We heard that there were clubs, just for women, where we could hear some music. Most of the gay clubs in the city were for guys and the lesbian bars were few and far between. We started frequenting one club out in North Hollywood called "Joanie Presents." A terrific gal, Joan Hanna, who was a drummer, ran it. She led an all-girl-all-lesbian band, and she and several of the other band members had been in the film *Some Like it Hot*. It was fun to listen to the music and to dance together and to feel like normal people. I began to notice that there was a lot of flirting happening at the clubs. There was always some dyke drama going on and sometimes, actual fights broke out over some cute new Femme on the scene or some Butch trying to move in on an established couple. Some of the other clubs were The Mint, Entre Nous and the Black Cat Tavern, which was mostly for the guys but lots of fun.

There was quite a bit of drug use going on in and out of the clubs. We started hanging out with several couples with whom smoking pot every day was a way of life. Mindy refused to try anything, but I had smoked pot in San Francisco when I was younger and enjoyed it, so I partook of a joint or two passed my way. There were a lot of parties that we went to, as we got deeper and deeper into the "scene." Soon Mindy joined.

PEYOTE DREAMS

One night, Roger, a gay friend of ours, had some peyote and suggested that we try it. I was willing, able and ready. Mindy refused and went to stay with her sister. She wanted no part of it. My daughter was with her father for the weekend, so it was a go! What I didn't realize was that part of taking peyote was the violent throwing up before anything happens. So, after throwing up pink stuff for what seemed like an hour, I began to see strange and wondrous things. As I drank a glass of water, a drop fell on the kitchen countertop. I was astounded by what I saw in that one drop of water. All of life was there. Movement of molecules, tiny creatures…all alive! Absolutely amazing! When I went to the bathroom and sat down on the toilet, it began speaking. It accused me of neglect. I was not doing a proper job of cleaning and what if I were it with all those asses sitting on me without a single thought of how I might feel…how I might want more attention paid for the service provided…. On and on it went, but this hallucination must have really stuck with me because, to this day, I probably have the cleanest toilet in L.A.

One of my favorite paintings is *The Girl With the Pearl Earring* by Vermeer. I had always loved the painting and had a print of it hanging over the pullout sofa. As I was peyote fixated on it, the beautiful young woman in the painting began to move. She turned her head toward me and said, "I was a servant girl in the household of a very wealthy family and Vermeer saw me one afternoon and asked me to sit for him. I was very flattered, and I agreed. As it took several weeks for the artist to complete the painting, I stupidly fell in love with him. The earring I am wearing belonged to Vermeer's wife and I was sure that he loved me since he took his wife's priceless earring for me, a poor girl, to wear. But alas, this great love was not to be as when the painting was finished, I went back to being a maid and had to return the earring as well!" The girl in the painting never knew she became famous, but I knew more than I had ever read about the painting and to this day believe I heard the truth.

After a few hours of marveling over the pattern of the rug on the floor, I moved into the front yard where I saw millions of tiny creatures in the grass, each going about their business with purpose. The bougainvillea was glorious in its beauty, each tiny flower perfect.

Roger came over to see how I was doing and suggested that we head out to the beach as morning was dawning. When we got there, I was stunned. Oh, my God! I could see the enormity of the universe in the waves, the water and the horizon that was dotted with shapes of ships or boats or meaningful blobs. The sun rose and the colors, the magnificence of our planet was overwhelming and staggering. These things that I saw and learned never lessened. I can certainly only begin to understand what the Native Americans, who use Peyote in their religious rites, experience. Mindy was interested in my experience but not for herself as she said she felt enlightened enough. "Yes, OK," I thought but I sure never met anyone who was "enlightened enough." But what the hell, she'll find out one of these days and it's not my job to tell her.

It was my one and only time to use Peyote. The gut-wrenching pink vomit part of the ritual kept me from ever trying it again. Still, I found it to be an overwhelming experience and believe that the power of it cannot be overestimated.

DALLAS AND AFTERMATH

1963

No one who was alive during that terrible day in November of 1963 will ever forget exactly what he or she was doing when they heard of the assassination of President John F. Kennedy. I had gone back to work at the insurance firm when I returned from Vegas and was working, transcribing some boring insurance details when the loudspeaker hanging from the shit-brown wall suddenly blared above my small cubicle. I took off my earphones to hear the life-changing news. We were first told that the President had been shot in the head while being driven in a convertible on a trip to Dallas. Then we heard the unspeakable. The loudspeaker blared. "We all mourn the passing of our President and due to this tragedy, we are closing the office until Tuesday, November 27th."

Everyone in offices all over America was sent home to mourn as a nation. I heard that some people in the South had cheered when they heard the news but, I think, for most of the country it was the end of a beautiful and hopeful era. We were glued to the TV for days as we watched the swearing-in of the now President Johnson on the plane, Jackie standing by in her bloody pink suit, her pillbox hat askew.

We watched the funeral as the horse drawn caisson went by, the horse with the backward-facing boot and small John saluting the plain wooden coffin. My daughter, who was sitting in my lap said, "Who's that little boy?" Mindy and I wiped away tears as I tried to explain in terms she would understand.

"The little boy," I said, "is the son of our President and he had a terrible accident, and the little boy is saying goodbye to his Daddy."

"Oh," she said. "I think that's sad. Is that why you're crying Mommy?"

I said, wiping away the tears, "Yes, my Puss, it's very sad."

We witnessed the assassin, Lee Harvey Oswald being shot in plain sight by Jack Ruby, a Dallas strip joint operator. The conspiracy theories still to this day debated, none of it ever to be forgotten. JFK, we found out as time went by, was not the perfect president or man, but it did seem that for one brief shining moment there was a Camelot, and we were part of it.

THE HAIGHT
1964

Mindy and I decided to take a trip to San Francisco to see for ourselves the scene we had been hearing about, The Haight-Ashbury district. Flower power was just beginning to blossom, and we knew a straight couple who had moved to Berkeley and said we could stay with them while checking out the action. I also wanted to show Mindy some of the sights of the beautiful town I knew so well from when I had lived there in the 50's. We arrived late on Friday, left my child with our friends who had a daughter the same age as mine, and went to town. I showed Mindy Vesuvio's where I had spent so much time with my friend Sally and next door the City Lights Bookstore owned by a fascinating man, Lawrence Ferlinghetti, who was the guiding light in the publication of "Beat" writers and poets, Ginsberg among them. I showed her where my parents and I had lived on Nob Hill and we went to Chinatown.

The next day we had breakfast with our friends and took off for The Haight. When I had lived in San Francisco the area was a crime-ridden neighborhood in decline. There were beautiful gingerbread Victorian homes that had been broken up into cheap apartments and rooming houses. The 19th century, multi-storied, wooden houses became havens for hippies and bohemians, artists and druggies. We wandered the streets

39

around the main drag, marveling at the out-in-the-open pot use and the colorful flowing garments the hippies wore. A young girl ran up to me and handed me a flower, "Power to the people," she sang as she stonily skipped away. Mindy said, "What people?"

I thought about it and said, "I think that's a slogan that the young people are using in protesting the war. If enough people speak up maybe the government will end the war." Viet Nam was becoming a boiling point and there had already been many young lives lost needlessly.

We had told Roger, the purveyor of peyote, that we were going to San Francisco, and he gave us the name and number of an "interesting" couple he knew whom he thought we'd like to meet. He said they were real characters, and we might get a kick out of them, so we found a phone booth, called them and were told to come on up. We found the run-down building, walked up several flights of stairs and knocked on the door. Hugely fat and slovenly, Ginny greeted us at the door holding a pipe and a glass of wine that she offered.

"Greet the day," she said. "Smoke a little weed and share a glass of vino. That's what life is." Since it was still morning, we declined and sat gingerly on a corner of a filthy couch, trying not to touch anything. The coffee table was littered with butts of partly smoked joints and several overturned bottles of wine. There was a baby crying in another room, but neither Ginny nor the nameless man who lived with her seemed to hear the plaintive wails. A combination of baby shit and weed pervaded the atmosphere and it was thick. The man took a toke on the joint he was holding and began a strange story.

He said, "Dig it now, hear what I'm puttin' down. Me and the old lady was sleeping, and we was woke-up by a powerful beam of light." At this point Ginny took over, "Oh my lordly, inside the beam was a creature, an ET, we guessed, and he slowly moved toward us." Nameless said, "The creature told us by, I reckon, his thought process to follow him. We was lifted up somehow, all afloat like and into one of those..." he hesitated, and Ginny said, "A UFO." "Yeah," he said. "A UFO. They was real nice to us." Ginny said, "They treated us with great respect and reverence! They showed us all around that thing, ship, whatever you want to call it, and then we just suddenly took off right into space." By this time, we were a captive audience. They went on sharing their remarkable adventure describing the colors they saw and the décor. They spent quite a lot of time communicating with the creatures that spoke to them through thought process, apparently a very efficient way of understanding one another. "Finally," Ginny said, "after a period or eon however long it was 'cause there really is no such thing as time, we were suddenly back in our own beds." They remembered specifically being told that there was to be a child and that the child would change the world, a messianic prophet who would lead the world into peace and perfection. Shortly after their return, Ginny. who was so obese that she didn't even realize she was pregnant, went into labor and produced a son who was now screaming in the other room. Finally, they seemed to become aware of the child and ushered us in to view the miracle.

He looked like any other baby, but Ginny insisted, "He

held up his head at two weeks and we can already tell he's way advanced mentally." We were not to see these advancements as she picked him up and rushed off to nurse him. When she returned with the now sleeping child, we took our leave promising to come again when the miracles occurred. As we left, I asked Mindy why she supposed Roger thought we would find those awful, sad, deluded people "interesting." She just shook her head. There was nothing to be said.

AGGIE

One night at "Joanie Presents" we saw and heard the great Aggie Dukes. She was a pianist and singer who had been trained in classical music but when we saw her, she was banging out rock and roll. By far her best number was "Georgia on My Mind." She sounded exactly like Brother Ray and the club went crazy when she really started rocking.

Aggie was six feet tall, dark coffee colored, with short hair and beautiful long hands. We became fast friends even though she had a really bad heroin habit. She once tried to get me to "skin pop" where you evidently stick the needle just under the skin to get high instead of injecting it in a vein. I declined since I was afraid I would like it and I vowed I would never do anything that might cause me to lose my precious little girl.

Aggie was busted once, went up to Chino. When I visited her, she said, "Girl, ain't you holding?" She was pissed off that when I kissed her hello, I didn't have anything in my mouth to pass to her. Evidently, it was pretty easy to get whatever you wanted in prison if you knew the right people.

One time, after she got out, she wanted me to drive her to her "connection." I should have said no, but again I put myself in a situation that could potentially be dangerous. We drove into South Central to a run-down housing development. The apartment was filthy, used needles on the floor, open bottles of cheap wine, unwashed dishes in the sink and lots and lots of roaches. The connection was a huge black dude with a bad attitude. Aggie told him, "Leave her alone, you hear me mother? She's a straight ofay."

He shrugged and said, "You cook?" I shook my head yes, terrified, and went into the kitchen to fix them something to eat out of what I could find while they "fixed." By the time I took them out some spam on white, they were on the nod and in no need of food. I sat down on the disgusting brown sofa, picked up an old copy of *Hustler* and looked at the semen-stained pictures until Aggie woke up and said we had to get out of there before Jamal came. I didn't ask who Jamal was, just ran out to the car as fast as we could and got out of Dodge. The whole episode scared me so much that I told her that in the future she would have to get another means of transportation if that was her destination.

She adored my daughter, and the feeling was mutual. The child liked to put her hand in Aggie's big one and one time commented, "Your hands are so pretty and they're all brown. How come you're that color?"

Aggie laughed, "Just lucky, I guess." She had a daughter back in New York whom she adored but because of her addiction was being raised by Aggie's mother. The girl was smart and years later after I had left the life, Aggie called me from New York. She had finally cleaned up and told me that her daughter had just graduated from college. She said how proud of her she was, and she wanted to know how my girl was. I told her that she was in college, doing well and that I had gone back to school and had become a teacher. She said she often thought of me and how strong I was that with all the junkies I knew and hung out with I had never used. I said it was because of my daughter that I stayed straight even though the temptation was enormous. We hung up. I never heard from her again but hardly a day goes by that I don't think of her.

UNDONE

1964-1965

With our new life in our safe and secure nest came unexpected problems. Mindy and I were on different tracks. Mindy had met a few people in the music business and had started playing her guitar and singing in several folk clubs in and around the Hollywood, Laurel Canyon area. She had a beautiful clear soprano voice and was really good. Out of one of these sessions she was asked to audition for The Young Americans, a group of singers who toured the country singing the praises of American Values and against the commie hippies who were protesting the war. She was accepted but turned it down so as not to leave us. In retrospect, I feel I should have encouraged her to go because I think her life might have turned out very differently. With Mindy's newfound independence and recognition, we were apart more that we were together and we began to have more arguments.

"Why won't you come with me to the coffee houses?" she asked.

"I'm just not interested in hanging out with a bunch of kids and listening to secondhand Judy Collins," I snottily replied.

"They're my friends." She whined.

Ramping up the argument I replied, "Well they're not mine and I have no interest. It's OK for you but no fun for me. Been there, done that!" She left, battered guitar case strapped on her back, and didn't come home until morning. She went into our room and closed the door. In the afternoon she came out carrying several bags and headed for the door.

"Just a minute," I said. "Where were you all night? What's going on?"

She stopped and said, "I've met someone who actually gives a shit about me and I'm moving in with her."

"What?" I managed to get out, "Who is this person? You can't just walk out on a three-year relationship."

She put the bags down. "This isn't a relationship," she said. "You don't love me and never did. I've had it with your high and mighty attitude. I was never an equal in your eyes. There was always something wrong with me unless we were in bed and that's changed too. I would have died for you, you know." She picked up her bags, walked out, got into her car and left.

I was floored. I had thought I was ready for my relationship with Mindy to end, but I was overcome with emotions I had never felt before. I called her every day, begging her to come back and got nothing. I promised her the moon, the stars, the planets, the universe if only she would come back. I was completely and utterly undone. I couldn't stop crying. I lost ten pounds and all my hair fell out. It was an effort to get out of bed. I honestly wanted to die. My boss at the insurance firm told me to straighten up or be fired. The fact that I knew from the beginning that it was bound to end badly was no balm for me. I honestly think that most of my angst came from the knowledge that she had chosen to leave me and that I no longer had any control over the situation.

Adding to the angst was the effect the breakup had on my child. I had been so selfish, wallowing in my own pain, I never thought of what she was going through. She was as devastated as I was, if not more. Mindy had been the only real mother she knew during those tumultuous years. She sat in my lap sobbing, "Why does everybody I love leave me?" I held her and promised I would never leave her, but the loss was so great, it was scant comfort to a bewildered little girl.

ELI
1964

As I began accepting the cold, hard fact that Mindy was really gone, I felt like I was floundering ... a fish out of water. It had been six months since Mindy and I broke up and during that time I just went to work, took care of my daughter and went to bed. It was all I could do just to get up every day. As the pain began to lessen some, I began to look elsewhere for companionship. I had very few friends, mostly from the clubs or friends that Mindy and I made who were couples and not open to continuing the relationship without Mindy, an unexpected and painful result of the split. I didn't know what I wanted or where to look for it. I was dissatisfied and antsy. I began to seek new adventure and excitement, ultimately sending me into a destructive downward spiral.

Carl and Carol were a straight couple I had met through Mindy's sister, and they welcomed me into their home and their lives. They lived in one of those fabulous bungalows between Sunset and Franklin. It had all the original features with built-in bookcases, a buffet in the dining room and the original kitchen. It was warm and cozy, and I loved being there. She was a homemaker and baker extraordinaire. He had some obscure job as an analyst — of what I never knew. They had a daughter the same age as mine and I often went over for food and conversation and for the girls to play. Much of our conversation was about art as they were avid collectors of emerging artists such as Ed Ruscha, Richard Diebenkorn and Donald Judd.

One night, Eli, a friend of Carl's stopped by and I was fascinated by this strange and interesting man who was to be an important part of my life, for a while anyway. He was thirty-eight years old and still lived with his mother in a small house near Plummer Park, now a Russian enclave but at that time heavily Jewish. Eli was corpulent, slovenly with sly humor and keen wit that somehow made him sexy, kind of like James Gandolfini. He was also a junkie. As far as I knew he never worked. It seemed that his mother had inherited a little money and she supported Eli and his drug habit. He openly used in the house and she moaned continually about it but continued to support him, as she loved him to obsession. He was her only child, the son of a renowned and venerated Rabbi, buried at Mt. Sinai Cemetery in its most sacred and holy ground, the greatest honor that could be bestowed upon any Orthodox Jew.

It was rumored that Eli had two doctorates and had had a nervous breakdown, which ultimately led to his drug use. He never spoke of this to me so I have no way of knowing whether this was true or not, but I was always a sucker for smarts and he was the smartest person I had ever met and, even when deep into his junkie dreams, Eli could expound for hours, if not days on any given subject. Our relationship was built on words not sex. We became very close pals. He never tried to get me to use and he didn't hang out with other junkies. All his friends were professional, mostly shrinks (go figure), and I think he did a little dealing in pot and pills on the side for his friends.

One day, Eli suggested that the two of us should get high on a psychedelic he called Romilar. He said it would be fun and since I trusted that he would take care of me in any given situation, and since it was my ex's weekend to take our daughter, I decided to go for it. We dropped the Romilar about 8 or 9 in the evening, had dinner with Carl and Carol and waited for it to come on. As we were waiting for what might or might not happen, I got the bright idea that we should drive to the Normandie Club in Gardena to play a little poker. Eli was not keen on this but off we went. We got on the freeway just as the Romilar started to hit. Oh my God! The lights, the billboards, the passing cars filled with leering faces were all too much overload on my now freaked-out brain.

"We have to get off here," I screamed. "I am freaking out. Eli, you have to get me the hell off this fucking freeway or something terrible is gonna happen."

Eli said, "We're in Watts and that's really not a cool place to get off."

I said, "Please, please Eli." He was not about to argue with a crazed drugged-out woman so off exit we went. "Stop the car," I screeched. "I have to get out of this car now!" Eli protested but turned onto a residential street. With my urging, he pulled over, parked and I jumped out like a cannonball.

By this time, it was probably midnight or after and the people were tucked safely in their beds of what, until then, had been a quiet black neighborhood. I should mention that due to an occurrence of Alopecia, I was as bald as a cue ball.

The damn wig I was wearing was so tight I thought my head was going to explode. I jerked it off, threw it on a well-manicured lawn and started running back and forth in front of the nice California style bungalows shouting, "The sky is falling, the sky is falling."

Eli tried to grab me as I ran past him. "Come on, we've got to get out of here, let's go!" he yelled. Now doors started opening with concerned black faces peering out at the bald white woman running up and down their nicely manicured lawns. Eli finally tackled me as I ran past a family standing outside in their PJ's. I heard the mother say something about a crazy white honky. Another yelled, "That bitch got no hair!" A third, "Sweet Jesus, save us from that she-devil!"

Eli started dragging me to the car. "My wig, where's my wig?" I asked as I made one last foray to grab it. Eli got me in the car and off we drove, hoping no gunshots would follow.

I was now going into the second phase of the "trip." I became terrified and the only way I could be appeased was to sit on Eli's lap facing him as we were frantically trying to get home, now made more difficult since Eli couldn't see the road. "You've got to lie down. If the cops stop us, they're gonna think we're two gay guys making out."

Since I knew somewhere in my addled brain that Eli was always right, I finally assumed a soothing fetal position on the old car's bench seat as we made the excruciating trip back to my apartment. I don't know how he was able to drive, but my guess is that Eli had taken so many drugs of every kind in his life that he probably wasn't able to get high himself anymore, so he got high watching others trip. By the time we finally got to my place, the "trip" was yellow mellow. I was fascinated to watch the walls melting and I really wanted to share my new insights with Eli, but he said he was exhausted and just wanted to go to sleep. The next day he said he had never experienced anything quite like that night and that he would never forget it. He never suggested "tripping" again.

When Eli turned 40, he decided to clean up. He went "cold turkey" and stayed straight for almost 6 months, but old habits die hard, and one night he thought he could have that one last shot before staying straight forever and it was his last. He had tried so hard, but he just couldn't withstand the power of the high. I was devastated. We sat shiva for three days and he was buried next to his father in hallowed ground with all the famous — and now one infamous — Jews.

THE ARTIST

One lazy afternoon, while having coffee and a delicious Bundt cake Carol had whipped up, an installation artist and assemblage sculptor stopped by to tell them about a new exhibit he was having at the then famous Ferus Gallery. He was an interesting man with an oversized ego, and although married, quite the ladies' man. As we happened to be leaving at the same time, he suggested that I should come up to his house in the canyon to discuss art further. Oh boy. Wouldn't you think that with all my worldly knowledge I would catch on to this old trick? But no, I was flattered and made a date for when I presumed his wife would be out of town.

On the appointed evening, I drove up to a large rustic rambling house and climbed the wooden railway ties to the massive handmade front door. He opened the door, invited me in, proffered a glass of wine and gave me a cursory tour of the house that ended in the bedroom. I actually was hoping to see some of his artwork or to be shown the studio where he did his constructions and to delve into his artistic psyche, but his only construct of the evening was to delve into me. I told him I was having my period so naturally I thought that would be a major turn off. I was wrong. In spite of my very vocal protestations, he threw me down on the bed, jerked up my miniskirt, tore off my panties and dove his face into my pussy where he grabbed my tampon with his teeth, pulled it out, looked up at me, bloody tampon hanging from his mouth, turned his head, threw the tampon across the room and began wildly fucking me as though I were a dog in heat. When he finished, he zipped up his paint-splattered chinos and left the room.

I was shocked, humiliated and bleeding. I put my torn panties on as best I could, went to the front door, slammed it, walked down all those railroad ties, got into my car, went home, got into a hot shower and went to bed. So much for art!

The year this happened was 1964 and I never told anyone until now what had occurred. At that time, if a woman was raped or groped or verbally abused it was assumed that she had "asked for it." If I had gone directly to the police station and asked for a rape kit (if they even had them then) they would have just laughed at me. What were you doing there? Did you have a drink? Why didn't you just leave? What were you wearing? Why didn't you just lie back and enjoy it? No, I sucked it up just like all the other women in that day and age. No jail time for the rapist artist, only castigation for the woman. Thank God we have come a long way in the long history of sexual harassment and rape.

JOJO

In my search for new adventures, I started hanging out at Joanie Presents on weekends when my daughter was with her father. One night, standing at the bar, I met JoJo. She was butch all the way: men's clothes, no makeup, hair buzz cut. The whole nine yards and good looking. She was quite a bit older than I, but she intrigued me.

We began a wonderful affair and I started to get bits and pieces of her life and soon I learned that she was the madam of a well-known house of ill repute in West Hollywood. Why did I stay with her when she revealed her profession? Any normal person would have hop skipped it out of there in a heartbeat, but I was fascinated. I didn't see the sordid side of her life, and then later the drug addiction. It was almost like voyeurism or an out of body experience, observing her and her lifestyle without being a part of it.

I found out that she had many famous people as clients. The most interesting one to me was one of my favorite actors whom I had watched in many fine films in the 40s and 50s. He always played the husband or father, a man you could turn to in times of trouble. A man everyone looked up to, a pillar of his community, in real life as well as reel life. I knew very little about the shadowy world of the sex trade, and was shocked to learn of his predilection for "The Golden Shower." On the days that JoJo was to see him she had to keep hydrated so she would be able to perform adequately. She never talked about any of her other clients, so I never knew of anyone else's pleasure or pain.

In the 50s she had been a professional seamstress and had made the clothes for the star of a popular children's show. I never asked her what had happened to so drastically change her life and she never volunteered any information. I never met any of the "girls" as she kept that part of her life separate, but I did see a rather unattractive, shoddily dressed woman having an argument with JoJo one afternoon and when I asked JoJo about it later, she said the girl needed money to "get well," which I took to mean drugs of some kind. The "girls" I met later dressed in designer clothes, were gorgeous and would have been canned by the madam if caught using drugs.

She regularly paid off the cops with cash and services performed by one or another of her girls. One time I was at her apartment, having a cup of tea, when a detective stopped by to collect. He sat down across from me, looked me up and down and said, "You know JoJo, I could really get into this piece of ass."

I was stunned and didn't know how to respond when JoJo spoke up, "She's mine Jack, not one of the girls so put your dick back in your pants and fuck off!" With that she handed him a fat envelope and escorted him out.

She was a wonderful lover, in fact, so good that no one since has made me feel the way she did. She was very kind and gentle but would never let me make love to her. She said her only joy in life was to please me. And she did. So much sometimes that when we'd be out, she'd brush my breast with her hand, and I would come. It was insane and wonderful. We went to all the clubs, gay and straight, where she was known and respected. In some of the clubs, her money was no good. "It's on us," either a patron or the owner would say.

A few of the gay clubs had dance floors where we could show off our moves. She was a fabulous dancer and we looked like professionals. I was having the time of my life. Everything was perfect with the exception that I had chosen another walk on the wild side. A normal woman would not, once she found out, stay with the madam of a whore house and a drug addict.

Some of her friends were pill heads. They downed Seconal and Tuinal like they were M & M's. She started using, a little at first then more and more until she was hooked. She knew I didn't use, and she tried to stay away when sick with craving and raving. Fortunately, I seldom saw her in that state. She met my daughter once and said how fortunate I was to have such a beautiful little girl. She said when she was younger, she had wished for a child, but she realized that there was no room for a child in the life she had chosen.

One day, after we had been together about three months, she called and said, "I have to go see my aunt whom I haven't seen in a long time and I'd like it if you would go with me." She explained that the aunt was getting pretty old and she thought she should visit her.

"Sure," I said. "I'd love to." She asked me to wear a dress and heels.

The appointed day came. I put on a nice dress and heels as requested but couldn't help but wonder what in the world

JoJo was going to wear since her usual attire was a suit with either an open collar or a tie. When I opened the door, I was astonished to see JoJo wearing a pretty flowered dress and nice heels. She wore a hat to cover her hair, lipstick and polish on her bitten down nails.

We drove out to Joshua Tree where her aunt lived in a small, snug house. She was a lovely woman in her mid-80s. JoJo introduced me. "Aunt Elva" JoJo said, "This is the friend I was telling you about. We met in church and have become good friends."

I was dumbfounded. "Oh, my goodness," I thought. "Where did she come up with that?"

Aunt Elva gave me a hug and said, "I'm so glad that Gladys has made such nice friends. It's so sweet of you to come all the way out here to see me." Gladys, I thought. My goodness.

"Well, Miss Elva, it's my pleasure. I've heard so much about you," I said, glancing slyly at 'Gladys.' Aunt Elva brought us tea and the chocolate cake that I had smelled baking as soon as we came into the neat and nicely furnished living room. We sat and talked for several hours. Aunt Elva asked me if Gladys had ever shown me her scrapbook. "What scrapbook?" I asked.

"Oh," she said, "Gladys has pictures of all the clothes and costumes she made when she was working for that nice woman on the TV.

Gladys just shrugged but I said, "Gladys, dear I would just love to see your scrapbook sometime. Maybe you could bring it to the church supper next week."

JoJo gave me a look to kill but said, "That's a great idea if

I can have some of that wonderful custard you make. I could just eat it all night." It was all I could do not to laugh out loud. The whole visit was bizarre, to say the least, but I was honored that she had asked me to go with her.

She thanked me profusely on the way home and said that none of her family knew of the life she really led. She was a gentle and loving companion, and I was devastated when she was busted for using as well as dealing Tuinal. She was sent to Chino, and I saw her a few times after she got back but the drugs had changed her, and we broke up. I never saw her again but heard that she had been seen around town in really bad shape. She had lost her business and her apartment and was living with some other junkies out in the desert. It broke my heart, but I have never forgotten the memory of that lovely afternoon with Gladys and Aunt Elva.

KIM RA KANE

As I delved deeper and deeper into the underbelly of the lesbian scene, I began to get farther away from any stability or sensibility. At one of the clubs, I met Sandy, a rich kid drawn into the life for the so-called thrill of it all. She seemed to have an endless supply of money and gave great parties at her cottage in Laurel Canyon. There was "Lady" as cocaine was known, bowls full of pills that looked like M&M's in all colors, shapes and sizes, poppers (amyl nitrate) mostly used for sexual enhancement when climaxing and pot, my only drug of choice. There were always a lot of off-duty hookers at these parties. Actually, they were too beautiful to be called by such a denigrating name. They much preferred "call girl" and they were always called "girls" never women. Most of these girls were from good families, some were in college hooking for extra money and some were just drawn to the life. It evidently was intoxicating to be paid so much money for so little effort. They each had a fee set by their employer, usually a woman, who had often been a hooker herself and who took a cut of the girl's take. These women were not pimps in the sense of some dude working the street trade. They also had nothing in common with JoJo, who although she was a madam too and had many celebrity clients, her "girls" were not of the quality, breeding and beauty as these girls. Their madams lived in beautiful homes/mansions, kept up an expensive lifestyle, stayed strictly away from hard drugs and got their "talent" through word of mouth passed from one girl to the next. The madam kept the Book, an indispensable and priceless list of the names and numbers of the Johns they knew. The more powerful and rich the client was, the higher the fee. At that time, it was several hundred just for a blowjob and the fees rose steeply after that. The top girls, who were the youngest, the freshest, the most beautiful, made thousands every week. There were sheikhs in Middle Eastern countries that arranged through the madam to fly in several girls for a weekend of debauchery at very high fees. The madams had strict rules about their clients' behavior and tried to protect the girls as best they could, but even the most powerful politician or movie star can have quirks and then would be promptly removed from the book if there had been any rough sex or harm to one of the girls.

I wondered when the girls got a little older what happened to them? Did the college girl graduate and become a lawyer? Did the heiress marry one of the wealthy men she serviced? Did some become junkies and end up on the street toiling for a pimp at twenty bucks a throw? I was drawn to these women and their stories. Again, as with JoJo, I was fascinated and intrigued by their lifestyles, so glamorous and exciting, I couldn't see the pain and suffering that would come at the end of their youth, their beauty, their fuckability. I was still standing back watching, but the flame was getting close enough to singe.

One night, Sandy told some of the invitees that there was to be a big surprise when we got to her house. We were all drugging, dancing, having a good time when in walks a very pretty girl whom, we found out, had just been released from Juvie for taking the rap for killing the gangster boyfriend of her very famous mother. She and her Juvie girlfriend had come straight to the party to celebrate. Years later I was thankful to hear that not only had she overcome the horrible and evil injustice she endured to save her mother's career, but that she had also become a highly successful businesswoman.

One of the most beautiful ladies of the night was Kim Ra Kane, who was absolutely gorgeous with an imperious and haughty attitude. She was Eurasian, I think, although no one seemed to know anything about her background. She was supposedly the top call girl in Los Angeles but again no one knew for sure. She was one of the few independent girls in town. She kept her own book, which was said to include some of the biggest names in Hollywood and elsewhere.

She had long, straight inky black hair, wore expensive clothing and carried herself like a model. No one knew how old she was, and it was said that she took a coffee enema every day as her beauty secret. She only appeared at private gatherings, always accompanied by a retinue of so-called Baby Dykes, all in their teens or early 20s. Sadly, I saw that Mindy had become Kim's favorite Baby. Evidently every girl that Kim took under her tutelage had to service her every night and was treated with disdain. By this time Mindy and I had long been separated but it still broke my heart to see her like that. No more dreams of being an artist, guitar forgotten or hocked. Her beautiful voice stilled.

Kim had a beautiful home in the hills above Paradise Cove

in Malibu and every weekend threw endless parties. One night I took my daughter to the daycare center that also provided night care and drove up Laurel Canyon where I parked my car in front of Christian's place. Christian was a hooker and junkie who ran with Kim and the other call girls. We got into her brand-new white Thunderbird and sped out to Kim's.

We had some food, got stoned, had some more food and pretty soon it was midnight, the witching hour for me. I announced that I had to go pick up my kid but there were no volunteers to drive me to the babysitter's house. They were all too comfortable, stoned and sated. I was on my own.

I walked at least a quarter of a mile to the bottom of the uneven gravel road to the Pacific Coast Highway and kept walking until I finally came to a bus stop in the middle of nowhere. At long last a bus came along, and I got on. For some stupid reason, I had gone out with no money, but the driver took pity on me and let me ride for free. He even gave me a transfer when we got to Hollywood for the next bus I had to take. That bus stopped across the street from a gas station at the corner of Laurel Canyon and Sunset Boulevard, still an uphill hike to my car. I pleaded with a gas attendant to take me up the hill and he was kind enough to do so. I finally got in my car and raced to the babysitter's house at what was now three AM. The sitter was, of course, pissed off and told me she couldn't keep doing middle of the night pickups and I would have to find someone else. There was also the matter of having a sleepy child who never should have been subjected to such an arrangement in the first place. It was a horrible experience, made less so by the generous kindness of strangers.

Later on I heard that Mindy had finally wised up and left Kim, was in a healthy relationship, painting again and trying to get into the music business. I pretended to myself that I was happy that she had found someone to love, but my senses reeled with the loss of her. I hadn't gotten over her and wouldn't for years to come.

CHRISTIAN

The job at the insurance company paid low wages so, of course, I was always broke. To save money Christian, who had been thrown out of her place, moved in with me as a room-mate. She was probably in her 40s although it was hard to tell because all the years of heroin use had aged her. She was junkie thin, blondish going-grey hair, with an ever-present cigarette hanging from her parched lips. She mainly kept to herself and that was OK with me. Like all the people I knew "in the life," she never fixed in front of me or, God forbid, my child. They all respected the fact that I didn't want to jeopardize losing my daughter and that I really wasn't interested in experimenting, as, by this time, I had seen too many young lives ruined by just "experimenting." So many people I knew died from ODs. Drugs have a way of stealing the soul, leaving the wreckage of lives once lived fully.

Christian had a standing John she saw every week that allowed her to keep up her habit with a little left over for rent and the payments on her beloved white T Bird. She spent a lot of time washing that car and inspecting it for any small scratch or dent. She hardly ever drove it except maybe if we were going out to a party at Kim's in Malibu.

One day she told me, "You know, I never told anyone this, but I wanted that car so bad that I called up a pimp who wanted to add to his stable and worked the streets downtown until I got enough for a down payment. I was a top call girl you know and doing that was really a comedown."

I was fascinated by her idea of success and asked, "What made you a top girl?"

She said, "Well, you wouldn't know it to see me now, but I was a hot piece of ass." She laughed, had a coughing spell and when she recovered said, "I looked a lot like Tuesday Weld. Did a real innocent act. Looked real wholesome, you know honey."

"Did that get you a lot of work?" I asked.

"Oh man," she said, "Every dick in town wanted to fuck me! I made a lot of money, but then I started using a little now and then for fun, you know. Oh, you know, it was so good. I guess it wasn't long before I was chasing the dragon just like every other junkie in this shit-ass-eating town."

She was always after me to make a little extra money by hooking. "You know," she said, "My john Charlie has a friend, an old guy like Charlie, wants a chick just to fondle his balls. No sex. He's up for a C note and on a regular basis." This notion wasn't exactly repulsive to me anymore as I had already fantasized about the "life". I didn't think too long about it before I said OK. Christian fixed it up and when the allotted night arrived, I dressed in my most alluring outfit and was ready to go.

About that time Christian's phone rang. "Yeah," she said. "No shit. What a bummer." She hung up, and said, "Well honey, you're off the hook. The old guy just had a heart attack and died."

I got the message. God had intervened. I started thinking

about my life and where it was going and my daughter's life. Was I really trying to be a good mother, or was she just an excuse to keep me from destroying myself?

CHANGE
1965

It finally dawned on me that I had hit bottom. It was a wake-up call. I was thirty-one years old. I had to change my life. Christian moved out and I tried to think of a way out of my situation.

I sent away for my credits from The University of Houston and discovered that I only had enough good grades to get me into a junior college. I started taking night classes to make up for the missing credits I needed to enter Northridge University. It was hard juggling studies with a job and a child. I managed somehow to pull it off and after a year was accepted to Northridge. I had decided that the best course of action was to try to become a teacher so that I would be available for my daughter during her summer breaks and holidays. I took as many courses as I could take and still be able to keep my job and hire a babysitter. It was hard work, but I had a goal and was determined.

Soon after my first year at Northridge, Mother came to visit. She had never accepted my lifestyle, but we had a relationship of sorts. She came with an offer. She and my father were proud of the fact that I seemed to be turning my life around and wanted to help me. I was to come live with them and finish college for which they would pay, and they would take care of their grandchild while I was in school. What a

Gift!

The only stipulation I had was that they were not to discipline my daughter, as I was worried that my father would try to control her as he had me. Nothing could have been further from the truth. They both loved and adored her and took better care of her than I ever had. I sold or gave away almost everything in my apartment except for the beautiful cross-cut oak dining table and six matching chairs I got for sixty-five dollars at the Salvation Army. That table weighed a ton and it sat in my mother's attic until I had finished getting my teacher's degree and found a place of my own. My daughter and I got on the train to a new life and never looked back.

As I was on the road to change, the country was changing also. Johnson began his full term as President. Martin Luther King and 25,000 civil rights activists, black and white, were able to complete their march from Selma, Alabama to the capitol in Montgomery. Johnson and Congress then passed a bill that finally allowed African Americans voting rights. On the advice of the Secretary of Defense, Robert McNamara, Johnson also sent more of our soldiers to Vietnam and by the end of the year there were over 300,000 combat troops in a never-to-be-won war. Young men started burning their draft cards and protests began in universities all over the country.

I was accepted at the University of Houston and began two years of an intensive, grueling course load to get a teaching certificate. There was little time for social activities and certainly none between my classmates and myself as I was, by far, the oldest student there. My parents gave me the luxury of a second chance in spite of all I had put them through, and I could never repay them for what they did though it seemed that just having their grandchild with them for those years was payment enough. They had changed in their attitude toward me now that I had some purpose. They valued hard work and "pulling one's self up by one's bootstraps" above all else and they saw me as a prime example of that.

I looked up a lesbian friend from the old Alley Theatre days and we hung out on the weekends when I had a little time to let off steam. She had a beautiful old house in the Montrose section of Houston and every Sunday gave parties. I danced many an afternoon away to Dylan's "I Ain't Goanna Work on Maggie's Farm No More." We had a great time and I struck up a brief relationship with yet another hooker, Patsy, known as Good Old Patsy, because if she liked the guy, she gave it away. She was sweet but I had too much work to play.

CHERYL

1966

Cheryl, whom I had known since childhood, was the perfect daughter of friends of my parents. She was also an only child and unlike me incredibly spoiled. When we were invited to their home for dinner, she was allowed to crawl around under the table while I had to sit still as a pin. She was very generous with her dollhouse though, which took up most of her separate playroom. She got an air-conditioned Caddy convertible when she was sixteen so needless to say I was terribly jealous.

Mother held her up as someone I should emulate, "Why can't you be more like Cheryl?" Why? Well, Cheryl was beautiful. Her curly and naturally blond hair formed a halo around her perfectly shaped face, light blue eyes and snub nose. She was rich and extremely smart. Her parents were from New Orleans originally and considered to be one of the best families. They spoke French among themselves and Cheryl was fluent. They were members of The Rex Organization in New Orleans which was founded in 1872 and its traditions have helped define Mardi Gras ever since. A King Rex is chosen from one of the leading families and at eighteen Cheryl was given the tremendous honor to be his Queen. She had invited me to come with her which was weird since we had absolutely nothing in common, but it was a nice gesture, and looking back I regret not going as it would have been exciting to go to all the parties and festivities. She graduated from a private high school with a 4.0 average and subsequently received two master's degrees and a doctorate from Rice University.

When I moved back to Houston, Cheryl called and invited me to join the top social club in the city. It was called Le Tres Gae! I was flabbergasted. Evidently, I heard, it was originally started by two lesbians as a safe place to meet other women of their social standing and sexual preference. There were meetings held with minutes kept, Robert's Rules of Order followed and beautifully dressed and coiffed women discussing current affairs. Cocktails were served and for certain members of the club discrete flirtations took place, usually after the meetings adjourned. To go on dates, you and the woman with whom you wanted to hookup had to have "beards," usually two guys who were members of a gay club for men who also had to protect their social standing. I accepted a date with a woman who was an executive with an oil company. She knew two guys who were going together, and one was her date and the other mine. Mine came to the house to pick me up. I introduced him to my parents who were thrilled that I had finally come to my senses. We then got in his Caddy convertible and drove off to meet my real date. Carol was a nice looking, somewhat older butch. At Le Tres Gae where we met, she wore beautiful and expensive clothes and had her hair styled in a short bob, suitable for the type of job she had. When the beard and I got to her apartment and rang the doorbell, we were greeted by a woman in jeans, a plaid shirt and cowboy boots. What a transformation. We had drinks and the beard went one way and Carol and I went to one of the very secret lesbian clubs in the Montrose district of Houston. When we got there, Carol was greeted as a regular customer. I met a few of her friends and we danced some but mostly we drank. I am not a drinker and no way could I keep up with Carol who glugged shots down like water. After a while of complete boredom, we went back to her apartment and made love in a room that had been decorated in her idea of a Moroccan tent. There were rugs on top of rugs and colorful curtains draped across every surface. She was too drunk to be a good lover and, as soon as I could, I left her softly snoring and got a cab home. I dated her a few more times but there was just as much dyke drama going on in Houston as in Los Angeles. The Montrose scene was alcohol and lots of it. I really couldn't keep up and also study, so I dropped out of Le Tres Gae and all activities associated with it. I never found out whether or not Cheryl was gay. She didn't marry until her late 30's and both she and her husband had top jobs with the space program. Mother sent me a copy of the obit when Cheryl died at fifty of ovarian cancer. We may not have had anything in common, but she was always very sweet and kind to me and I was sad to see that her full and productive life was cut short so early.

BEGINNINGS

My little girl just blossomed under the care and love of her grandparents. I was a distant figure in her life as I was busting my ass studying, trying to keep up with kids ten years younger than I. I began to realize that if I were ever going to be a mother and take on that responsibility, now was the time. As much as I could, I played with her, read to her and rocked her to sleep singing, "Someone's in the Kitchen with Dinah" and "You Are My Sunshine." My love for her was boundless and I tried to show her in ways I never had before. She was a happy little girl and when her Theo came to Houston to work again at The Alley and to try to reconcile with me, she was excited at the thought that we might be a family again. My grades started improving and by the time I graduated, I had made the Dean's List! My parents were thrilled, and my attitude and persona began to change. I didn't want to return to the life I had led. Theo convinced me that we could make a go of it and in 1968, we remarried, only to divorce again in ten years, but that's a whole 'nother story and not one to be told here.

When I returned to live with my parents, I was quite ill. Besides the Alopecia, I had lost a lot of weight, was anemic and had developed Hypoglycemia. My father took me to see his doctor and by the time I started school, my hair had started growing back, and the Hypoglycemia was controlled by following a strict diet. My father was the one who took care of me. He cooked for me, cleaned up after me when I was sick and did it all without any complaint or recriminations. One day I said, "Daddy, I want to know why you've never said you were sorry for your abusive behavior towards me when I was a child?" He just looked at me and with tears running down his face said, "I would do anything if I could only take all that back. I am so sorry...so sorry." By then I was crying. I tried to forgive him, but the pain still lingered like a sore that wouldn't scab over.

Mother did nothing for me but, in her devotion to her granddaughter showed me that she was capable of love, althhough it seemed to have skipped a generation.

During those months of rest and recuperation, I began to realize that I since I was the progeny of two incredibly dysfunctional people who had no idea how to have a healthy relationship or how to be good and effective parents, I had to teach myself to be a good person, live by the rules, be more responsible. It had not been possible for them to teach me what it takes to be a fully integrated person because they were on cruise control themselves. I came to understand that my father's abuse certainly affected my relationships with men and between his personality disorder and Mother's narcissistic behavior, it's no wonder that I strayed into dysfunctional relationships, irresponsible behavior and risky escapades.

I tried to remember if there had been any girls or women I had been attracted to before Mindy. There was a girl in high school that had wanted to be more than a friend. At TSCW, as a freshman, there were women who came on to me, but I was not interested. I finally came to the realization that although I have gotten more sexual and emotional pleasure and certainly learned a lot about myself from Mindy and the several other wonderful and loving women with whom I had affairs...women just weren't my thing, or were they?

For the men in my life, I had always been attracted to the bad boys...those who lived on the edges of life. I chose Theo whom I thought would be a stabilizing influence. In him I saw a good man who would take care of me and keep me on the straight and narrow...a Good Daddy if you will, only to discover that his insecurities were as great, if not greater, than my own. I also found out that Theo was, in some ways, a lot like my father. He was a rageaholic and could be emotionally abusive by constantly putting me down. Since the major male role model in my life had a severe personality disorder, it seemed I had no other choice but to keep looking for men with those same characteristics.

And what about Mother? I always had a particular girl-friend who was remarkably pretty, vain, selfish and narcissis-tic...all traits of Mother's, and interestingly those of my hero-ine, Scarlett O'Hara. These girls and later women treated me in the same manner that Mother had, giving me attention, affection, and excitement then taking it away. Of course, any psych would say I was chasing after Mother's love with these impossible relationships, and yet I just kept forming the same pattern. Were these crushes sexual in nature? If anyone had even suggested such a thing at that time, I would have been horrified and disgusted. So, what happened to change that?

There was only one place to look for answers...I had to go back. I had to go back to the beginning.

FATHER

1901-2000

My father was born on a farm in what was then the bustling sugar cane town of Sugartown, Louisiana. When he was sixteen his father was injured while working in the local sawmill and was disabled. My father, being the eldest son of seven children, had to quit school and go to work to support the entire family. I believe that having to give up such important years in a young man's life hardened him and made him the taskmaster he later became. He held many jobs during this period from cutting hair for a quarter to shipping out of New Orleans to work as an engine wiper on a ship that went back and forth to Venezuela. He talked about how the other men, once they hit port, would head for the nearest bordello but he prided himself on his restraint in such matters, as he needed every hard-earned dime to support his family and to save some money to go back to school. His dream was to become an engineer and to that end he spent many an hour of what little leisure time he had learning to draw mechanical engineering plans that he learned from a book. When his siblings were old enough to help out, he was finally able to finish high school and be accepted to LSU as an engineering major. He was only able to finish one year of college since the only subject in which he excelled was his self-taught mechanical drawing. With no college degree and only one skill, he was somehow able, at the height of the depression, to get a job as a draftsman at a small chemical company in Houston.

MOTHER

1909-2012

Mother's life changed completely in 1918, when her father took the wagon with the cotton crop to the cotton gin, sold the cotton, went to the store, paid off the years' debts, went to the train station, left the wagon and horses and disappeared, abandoning a wife and seven daughters. None of the sisters ever talked about that time, but they must have been so frightened. I can't imagine what they had to endure when the man who, up to that time, had been a loving man, a good father and a hard worker, abandoned them to an uncertain future or no future at all without a backward glance. Later, when they were grown, my aunts Agnes and Ada were shopping in downtown Houston when they thought they saw their father. They dismissed it as an illusion but when my cousin Ronald was researching the family tree, he discovered that our grandfather had remarried and had several children by his new wife. A bigamist!

My grandmother was not in any position to run the farm with just her and the girls, so she accepted the offer of a widowed neighbor to take care of him in exchange for room and board. He erected a tent in his field, laid a tarp for ground cover, pallets to sleep on and they lived there for four years. He also provided material so my grandmother could make clothes for the girls.

She probably slept with him in gratitude and maybe a little human warmth. I can't imagine the pain and suffering they all endured during that time, but it certainly affected each of them differently.

When Mother was very old one day, she said she would never forgive her mother for what she did. I knew what she was talking about, all those years ago when Grandma had probably slept with the widower. I looked at her and said, "Did you ever think that she did what she did to keep all you girls together? If she hadn't done that all of you would have been farmed out or made wards of the state." It took a minute or two to sink in...then...." Oh my God, I'm so sorry." Too little, too late.

The smartest and prettiest of all the girls, Mother was the hardest hit by her father's abandonment. She was nine years old when he left and absolutely adored him. I believe she thought he loved her more than her sisters and by leaving took all her love with him. In my opinion she never grew up and had no capacity for real love or an emotional life. When questioned about her father, she refused to answer except once, in her hundredth year, she said, "If he walked into this room right now, I would spit on him!" She never cried that I saw, couldn't watch emotional films or listen to sentimental music. When my father died after seventy-two years of marriage, she never shed a tear.

When she graduated from High School, she was able to get a scholarship to a two-year college in San Marcos, Texas where she gained a degree to teach elementary school. She was very popular due to her beauty; dark curls framing an oval face and lovely dark eyes. She had spunk, intelligence and a sharp wit that was intact until the end of her long life. She dated fellow student Lyndon Johnson a few times.

"Gee, Mom. Really? What was he like?"

"I don't remember," she said. "Just that he always spoke highly of his mother." When she graduated, she taught at a two-room schoolhouse in the German and Czech part of Texas outside of San Antonio. In the 1840s many Germans and Czechs moved to the Hill Country where they sought to improve their economic conditions by farming. Mother taught first grade through sixth and the other teacher seventh through twelve.

MARRIAGE AND FAMILY

It was the late 1920s and most of Mother's sisters had moved to Houston either with their husbands or to work. During the summer when school was out, Mother would go to Houston to work and live with one or the other of her sisters. It was the second such year when my father brought his newly purchased clothing to be pressed at a local cleaning establishment and met Mother who was working behind the counter. He was smitten the minute he laid eyes on her. She was not smitten but did know that she would make the perfect wife for an up-and-coming young engineer, and in 1930 they were married in a small ceremony.

My father was a hard worker at the plant and was soon promoted from draftsman to supervision over the other draftsmen and then taken out of the office to supervise some of the men working with the toxic chemicals. He was good with the men but made them toe the line and get the work done on time and that impressed his bosses.

My parents' early marriage seemed to be a happy one, from what I heard. Mother loved to dance, and my father was so in love with her that he was willing to do anything to please her, even to take her to the band pavilion to dance though he could never do more than the two-step, sometimes called the Texas stomp.

In their long life together, he tried one way or another to

please a woman that didn't love him and could never be pleased, since for her it was always a marriage of convenience, not love. She was astute in her ability to get what she wanted and could turn on the charm like a lightbulb. She saw a man with ambition, and she knew how to keep the flame of that ambition burning. She was the very essence of the woman behind the throne. She knew how to present herself and her marriage to the outside world. All their friends spoke of how happy they were, what a beautiful couple. She entertained as lavishly as was affordable, bringing people to the table who could help my father get ahead. She knew how to maximize every encounter to her advantage. In her private life, she drew friends toward her like a magnet, using them and then dropping them without a thought. In late life, she had a friend, Bernice, who adored her and would actually get up at the crack of dawn to take her to Urgent Care. When Bernice passed away suddenly, I called Mother to offer my condolences, only to be told, "Oh, yes…well, I never liked her much anyway!" As I was growing up, I watched this behavior with a mixture of horror and envy. I was never able to get the attention she so lovingly bestowed on others, but I did get the dropping part.

THE ONLY CHILD
1934-1941

I was born in Houston four years after my parents married. I was an only child, and it was my daddy that made up my whole world. Six feet tall, thin, some would even say willowy. My father had brown eyes with a green rim around the iris, so they sometimes looked green, just like mine. He liked to be well-groomed, shaved close with a straight-edged razor, which he sharpened every day with a razor strop that was always kept in a prominent place, which was easy to get to or later to grab. He always smelled of Old Spice and was a very handsome young man. He never smoked or drank for which he took great pride. Every Sunday he held me on his warm, scratchy woolen lap to read the funny papers out loud. He was very affectionate, hugging and kissing me, and the only time I ever remember being spanked, at least at that time, was the day I decided to ride my brand-new red tricycle off of the sidewalk and into the street. My daddy, who had been proudly watching me whiz by, yelled for me to stop. I was not a stopping little girl. I jumped off that trike like a flea off a dog and started running as fast as my four-year-old chubby legs would let me, but I couldn't outrun Daddy. When he finally caught up to me, he jerked me up and spanked me sharply on the bottom of my pretty little yellow ruffled panties. I started bawling and he hugged me, told me he was sorry, but it was bad to go into the street. I stopped crying, got back on my trike and rode as fast as I could next door to show my boyfriend, Sonny, my new trike. That going in the street had been a dangerous thing never entered my mind. I'd had fun, outwitted Daddy and the spanking didn't connect, in my mind, with the act itself.

Sonny had snow-white hair and dimples and wore cute little rompers, mostly blue to match his eyes. I liked him because he would do anything I wanted, a trait I have always found desirable in men. His mother and mine were best friends, and they spent a lot of time gossiping, which I guessed ladies did. Sonny lived in a red brick house like most of the other houses in our neighborhood, but Mother wanted a big white house, so Daddy made it for her. It was a beautiful, two-story white wooden house with a white picket fence right out of the Ladies' Home Journal. Daddy had bought the lot because it was just down the block from my Aunt Essie, Mother's favorite sister and my favorite aunt. The house had two bedrooms, a dining room and a big living room with a fireplace.

For Mother, who had lived in a tent after "The Abandonment," to actually live in her very own house must have been beyond her wildest dreams, and she was the queen of her domain. She kept that house spotless, and God forbid if I didn't pick up my toys or keep my room tidy, which for a four-year-old wasn't the easiest task, but I did it for the praise that never came. I have no memory of her hugging or kissing me. In fact, she hardly ever touched me, and since I never got any affection from her, a lifelong affliction, I really didn't miss it until

I was older and really needed some motherly advice; but I had to look elsewhere. As a prime example, when I got my period at fourteen, I thought I was bleeding to death. I ran into the kitchen screaming, "Mama, something's going on down there, I'm all bloody!"

Mama said, "Come on." She took me to the bathroom I had just vacated, opened the cabinet and handed me a box containing a thick white rectangular pad with little ties on each end. She said, "You've got the curse. Clean yourself and put this in your panties and stop whining." Curse! Why? What?

I called my girlfriend, Marion, who knew everything. She said she'd explain everything the next day at school. When we met in the girls' bathroom, Marion took a box of Kotex and a sanitary belt out of a bag. She showed me how to attach the pad to the belt. She explained the whys and the whats of the menstrual cycle, said it was perfectly normal, gave me a kiss and said, "Congratulations, you are now officially a woman."

A real stunner, Mother was slender with a small waist, beautiful breasts and lovely legs that she considered to be her best feature. She loved to have a good time, maybe a cigarette once in a while, a drink on occasion. She had naturally curly hair that, unfortunately, I didn't inherit, and my stick-straight hair seemed to be just one more thing about me that annoyed her. When I was four, she took me down to Foley's department store and demanded a perm that would make me look like Shirley Temple. Fat chance! First of all, I had dark brown hair, was tall for my age and certainly didn't have a button nose. It was awful. First, they rolled what little hair I had on these rod curler things. Then they poured this rotten egg smelling stuff on the rods which had long wires attached to some kind of electrical contraption that I had to sit under for an eon. Then, finally they undid the rods and washed my hair. When it was over my hair did fall in ringlets, and even I thought it was an amazing transformation. Mother seemed very pleased. We went downstairs, stepped into the Houston mugginess and my hair fell completely out of its beautiful ringlets and turned straight as the stick it had been. Well, Mother was nothing if not determined so back we went upstairs, where she insisted they do it all over again. It was a true wonder my thin hair didn't fall out with all the chemicals poured on it and maybe some leached into my brain; that would certainly explain some of my weirder tendencies. This time it took even longer but with the same sad result…beautiful ringlets then, bam, stick hair. Well, that did it. She jerked me back to the car, drove us home and from then until I was a teenager, she braided my hair every morning, a very painful operation that I believe was painful on purpose, pulling my hair and jerking my head back and forth. The braids were so tight I had a headache every day until she finally let me have my hair cut short when I was twelve.

In the attic there was a large room that was my playroom and also a guest room if anybody came for a visit. The only person that I ever remember staying there was my Grandma whom I loved with every pore in my being. I loved the way she smelled like the snuff she chawed and the way she could spit across the room and hit her spit jar dead on. I loved the large mole on her chin with three bristly hairs growing straight out from it that was all tickly and scratchy when I rubbed my pudgy little cheek against it. She held me and rocked me and told me she loved me like the mother I never had. I think my Grandma knew her own daughter well and understood the reasons for the anger, hatred and lack of love. Mother was ashamed of her and treated her as she might have a servant, and when we had company Grandma was sent up to the attic like Rochester's crazy wife.

Years later when she died and we were living in San Francisco, I refused to go to her funeral as seeing her in the open casket would have broken my heart. So, she came to see me. I was just lying on the couch in the den when I sensed and smelled something, and there in the living room up on Nob Hill my Grandma materialized. She told me that she loved me and by the time I had gotten up to run to her, she'd vanished. I really believe it happened as the sweet smell of snuff lingered for a while.

One day Daddy came home with news. He was being transferred to Fort Worth to become the superintendent of a chemical plant there. It was a big promotion but caused uproar in the household. Mother's beloved sisters all lived in Houston or nearby, and she just absolutely wouldn't leave them or her beautiful house to live in some awful old dump on the grounds of a plant in the middle of nowhere, and she just threw a hissy fit. It was the most honest display of emotion I had ever seen from her and I was impressed, but Daddy was not. I'm sure she used all the ammunition in her arsenal, including sex, to get her way, but at any rate none of it worked, or maybe it did, because after we moved everything in my life irrevocably completely and forever changed as I watched and experienced my wonderful and loving Daddy transform himself into the devil.

FORT WORTH
1941-1952

The move to Fort Worth was a promotion for my father and an important one for the war effort from 1941 through 1945. The plant he supervised made hydrochloric and sulphuric acid and he was given the much-coveted E for effort for producing in volume the dangerous acids that were considered indispensable for the production of jet fuel, steel manufacturing, explosives and nerve gas. The pressure of running such a huge plant coupled with my mother's unhappiness turned him into a completely different person from the wonderful Daddy I had so loved.

The house we were given to live in was an ugly red brick building that was separated from the plant by a large open space. It was Mother's worst nightmare. We were surrounded by two hundred acres of nothing but hay and were really out in the country with nowhere to go and nothing to do. Father decided that Mother should have a horse to help quell her unhappiness, so she got a very nice mare named Bonny. We also had a cow, Bossy, Bully the bull, chickens, ducks, twelve cats and my only friend, Shep, a German Shepard.

Bully was given to me to raise. That bull followed me everywhere. He, Shep and I were inseparable. What I wasn't told, which wasn't surprising, was that I was really raising Bully for them to slaughter. One day Bully disappeared, and the following week we had meat on the table. When quizzed about this, my parents insisted that Bully was alive and well and had been sold to live peacefully on a large farm. Well, I may not have been the brightest bulb in the chicken coop, but I knew where that steak on the table came from and I refused to eat Bully until there was no more meat on the table.

Father had evidently wanted another child, but since Mother wasn't about to have another kid, he tried to make me into the son he was never to have. I was a complete failure at hunting, riding, frog gigging, fishing, sports of any kind and all the other things young Texas boys at that time learned and seemed to love. I was a very girly girl and loved my paper dolls, reading fairy tales and sneaking into my mother's bookshelf where forbidden delights awaited.

It must have been a terrible disappointment to my father that I didn't live up to his expectations. Maybe he saw it as rebellion or stubbornness on my part or maybe the lurking rebelliousness that was part of my nature. But for whatever reason he began to whip me over infractions of the rules. What these rules were I never understood because it seemed as if the smallest thing would set him off. I didn't shoot the rabbit when I had a perfect aim, or I refused to go fishing with him when he turned over the boat and seemingly millions of water moccasins slithered out.

It started soon after we moved, when I was six. I could hear him coming after me, the Old Spice emanating from my father like the poison gas he was helping to make. At first, I tried to get away but soon learned that was of no use, so I stood as still as a moss-covered rock in my orthopedic oxfords waiting, my stomach clenched in fear and dread. The whippings always happened in the hallway between the two bedrooms where the stairs to the attic hung above me like Damocles' Sword. He would go into the bathroom and grab the razor strop, leather shined and ready for stropping or strapping. Down and down it came, over and over, on my butt and legs.

Sometimes if the infraction was serious enough, he would whip off his belt with a loud snap and whop me on the backside. One time, in an effort to stem the pain, I shoved a pie pan down my pants but as soon as he heard the twang of the pie pan and not of the flesh, he told me to get that goddamned pan out of there, and as soon as I did, the belt was relentless in its pursuit of pain. No matter how good I was, he seemed to find some reason to whip me. Maybe I realized that, since it didn't seem to matter whether or not I was good, why bother? And where was Mother during those years? Good question, and one that remained unanswered even when she finally came to my rescue.

After a few years I stopped crying. There just weren't any tears left. My father had won and without even trying had beaten me down, destroying my self-respect, my self-worth and hope. The few times I tried to stand up to him I was beaten with even greater wrath. "You think you can sass me little girl? You'll wish you never opened your goddamned sassy mouth when I'm through with you." I wished him death every day and thought nothing of it.

One night I thought my prayers had finally been answered as in the middle of the night he ran out of the bedroom yelling, "Black Widow bit me! Black Widow bit me!" There were many of these nasty spiders that were always skittering around the house. My mother, who was laughing so hard I thought she might fall off the bed, said, "Oh shut up old man. You were snoring so loud I stuck you with a pin." He was so relieved that he wasn't dying he didn't even yell at her.

SCHOOL
1941

Diamond Hill Elementary was the first school I went to. I loved it there. Most of the kids' parents worked at the plant or the stockyards down the hill, fortunately downwind of us. In my very first stage appearance I played Uncle Sam in a school play about acceptance of all the immigrants in our country. There were many children there whose parents were from different countries and each child wore his or her native costume when they came on the stage to be welcomed by Uncle Sam. I shook each hand and welcomed them to our wonderful country. My first-grade teacher Mrs. Murphy was kind, and my always-good behavior was rewarded by A's on my report card. My mother, however, looked down on these "lower class people." She was always going on about the poor white trash as though she herself had not been a member of that same group not so very long ago.

I was excited to learn that my third-grade class was going on a field trip. I imagined the ice cream factory or a bakery but no, this was after all Cow Town, so our teacher marched us to the stockyards to witness how the cows were killed. We stood on a balcony overlooking the kill zone. We all watched in horror as the cows were sent down a long chute, headfirst all the while making horrible noises. When they reached the bottom of the chute there was a guillotine-looking contraption, which decapitated them very efficiently. Then, workers in hip boots hauled the still twitching cow torsos across the shit and blood covered cement to throw each body into a pile of other cow corpses. What fun! The workers looked up at the eight-year-old children gasping in fright and waved at us. We waved back. I couldn't sleep for weeks without seeing those poor cows sliding to their doom, their cries unheeded.

THE SWIMMING LESSON
1943

When I was nine, my father decided that I should learn to swim. Out in the back of the property near the outhouses and stables there was an old acid-cooling tank that had been cleaned and filled with water. It was fifteen feet long, eight feet wide and thirty feet deep. One sunny June morning, my father told me to put on my swimsuit, took me out to the tank and said, "Jump in." Jump in, I thought. What is he talking about? I'll die if I jump in there!

This time he yelled, "Jump in the goddamned tank before I whip you!" Scared to death but more afraid of him, I jumped in and sank straight down, then bobbed up sputtering and terrified. I was on my way to the bottom again, but my father seemed to take no notice that I was drowning right in front of him. He was actually standing there watching me go down again to the depths of hell while he stood there and yelled, "Swim, God damn it, move those arms and legs!" I was too scared to do anything but wildly flail about in the cold water. Finally, on the third time down a hook was proffered which I grabbed for dear life, and he pulled me to the rickety ladder attached to the tank and I got out. I ran screaming and crying into the house fearing that he was really trying to kill me. Mother, as usual, paid no attention to my protestations and just said, "Get that swimsuit off, you're dripping on my clean floor."

Foolishly, I thought that having almost drowned me, Father would surely realize that I was not meant to swim. Not the case. The next day the same ritual: swimsuit on, jumping in, drowning. This horrible tradition went on for years, him yelling at me to swim and me nearly drowning. I began to have a recurring nightmare. I was sitting in the front seat of a large black hearse with a man who looked like Abraham Lincoln or maybe it was my father in a tall hat. We drove down an endless road and into water that crept higher and higher until I woke up gasping for air. The man who freed the slaves had done nothing to save me. He only turned away humming, "We are gathered at the river...the beautiful, beautiful river..." That this was the only song my father ever sang could have been coincidental, but I had that dream until I finally learned to swim in college.

In retrospect, I think he was trying in his own insane way to toughen me up for the "real" world that had been so hard on him, although, at that time it certainly didn't toughen me up...it just made me fearful of whatever that "real world" might be.

THE WAR
1941-1945

I was six years old when the war started and was too young to really know what was going on, but soon I noticed that things began to change. My parents were issued ration books that contained removable stamps good for certain rationed items, like sugar, meat, cooking oil, lard, canned goods, cheese, butter, coal, firewood, nylons, silk, gasoline and the list went on and on. When you went to the store you had to give stamps for any rationed item when you checked out.

We had what was called a Victory Garden where we grew tomatoes, beans, peas, greens, potatoes and other necessary food items tended by our indispensable handyman, Mr. Smith. We were more fortunate than most, and because of our cow and chickens, we had fresh milk and eggs every day. Everyone had to pitch in and one of my chores was to churn the fresh cream into butter.

The children were encouraged to save aluminum foil from gum wrappers and cigarette packs to make into big balls. It was always fun to see who could make the biggest ball. String and newspapers were also saved as well as tin cans and other metal.

School always started off with The Pledge of Allegiance to the Flag and a prayer for those in the military. We were given updates on how our military were winning over the dreaded

Nazis or "Krauts" and the "Dirty Japs," or "Yellow Peril." We thought nothing of using such demeaning words as we were at war and anything goes. We were taught propaganda songs that we sang in school. Some of them were: "We'll Knock the Japs Right into the Laps of the Nazis," "Der Fuehrer's Face," and "Praise the Lord and Pass the Ammunition," a personal favorite of mine. The school held a fair to raise money for some of the children whose parents couldn't afford to buy shoes, one of the rationed items. My mother bought a raffle ticket and lo and behold won a pound of sugar. One would have thought it was a million dollars, as sugar was especially hard to get even with a ration ticket. We had cake and pies again for a while.

By 1945, the war was winding down, and we were all elated to be winning in Nazi Germany and thrilled to have the "Japs" on the run. On April 12th of that year, I was in the kitchen shelling peas, listening to *Let's Pretend* on the radio, when a newscaster broke into the program announcing that President Franklin D. Roosevelt had just passed away. My mother stopped ironing and ran from the room. She was a supporter unlike my father who referred to him as "That Jew!" My father was always going on about the "Jews." He blamed most of the ills of the country on the bankers and the rich whom he thought were all Jews. It was strange because their best friends were Jewish, and they spent a lot of time hanging out with them, going on trips to Vegas to gamble or to the horse races in Louisiana. It was a sad day for most Americans because, among other things, during his presidency The Social Security Act was passed which ensured that all of us would be taken care of when we got old. It didn't exactly work out that way, but it sure helps.

SUMMERS

I never thought about why I was sent away every summer. Maybe it was to give me time with my extended family or maybe just to get rid of me for three months. I don't know and never asked but it was heaven for me. Every June, I was taken to the train station, put on the train, and sent by myself to Houston, where I was met by one or another of my many relatives. They were all wonderful people and I eagerly awaited summer so I could live for a little while with real families who were loving and kind. On my mother's side there was Aunt Ada who made me learn a bible verse before I could go to sleep, Aunt Lois who was raising two boys on her own, Ronald who was my age and Nathan. My Aunt Tip was the most fun, Aunt Agnes, and Aunt Essie, my very favorite. She was round and huggable and, I thought, loved me just as much as she loved her spoiled son, Donald. Uncle Emmitt was also round but definitely not huggable. He had two chihuahuas, Sampson and Delilah that went everywhere with him and seemed to always be stretched out on his spacious lap. Every time I'd get anywhere near them, they'd growl and snarl with my uncle egging them on, "Sic her, Sampson. Go get her Delilah." It was great fun for him but not so much for me.

Aunt Essie had the Amazing Electric Mangle. It was an ironing machine. Uncle Emmitt had to have fresh, ironed sheets every night, so he bought her the machine for Christmas one year. She loved that machine and used it almost every day. My job was to hold the end of the sheet off the ground so it wouldn't get dirty. I enjoyed helping her because she always made every job fun. She liked to pretend too, so we'd be secret agents or spies or something. It was such a change from my home of no love or fun and certainly no hugs.

Aunt Essie was kind to everyone. She went to the Baptist Church near where they lived and I would go with her, sit in the hard-wooden pews and sing hymns. I loved "What a Friend We Have in Jesus" and "I Walk in the Garden Alone." Aunt Essie enrolled me in Vacation Bible School, and we read scripture and sang songs. I enjoyed "Jesus Loves Me, This I know for the Bible Tells Me So" and "Jesus Loves the Little Children." In the song the lyrics go:

> Jesus loves the little children,
> All the children of the world,
> Red, and yellow,
> Black and white,
> They are precious in his sight.
> Jesus loves the little children
> Of the world.

I really took the words of that simple hymn to heart and believed that, like Jesus, we should love all the peoples of the world no matter what color they were. I soon discovered that even in my small world that was not the case. As my consciousness grew, I became more aware of the ugly words I heard all around me. Catholics were papists and had actually killed Christ. Jews were thieves and liars. All around me was the worst kind of hate and prejudice coming out of the mouths of seemingly good Christians. It was confusing to an 8-year-old, but somehow, I knew it was wrong and vowed to never use any of those hurtful words.

When we had supper, Uncle Emmitt had to have his dessert first. He said that he was afraid he might have a heart attack during supper and would be dead by the time dessert arrived. He actually did die of a heart attack, but I don't know whether he got his dessert first.

Every night after supper, Aunt Essie would draw a bath for Uncle Emmitt. I didn't understand why he couldn't do this himself, but my Aunt seemed to think it was her duty. She would kneel on the fluffy rug she put by the side of the tub and begin to scrub his back. She washed him all over like he was a baby. After the bath he would go to bed as he had to get up really early to go to work, and my Aunt and I and sometimes Donald would listen to the shows on the radio. My favorites were *Fibber McGee and Molly* and, of course, *The Bob Hope Show*. When I was home, we had to listen to *The Lone Ranger*. Hi Ho Silver, Away! It was on at dinnertime and no talking was allowed during the show, not that any of us had anything to say anyway. I sent away for the secret decoding ring from Captain Midnight, but didn't learn to decode anything.

On my father's side there was Aunt Gladys, Uncle Clifford, Uncle Cloyce, Uncle Everett and Uncle Woody. I loved going to Louisiana to visit Aunt Gladys and Uncle Bill, the most lovable man who ever lived, and their three kids, Edith Gale, Billy and Charles Lee. My parents and I usually went at Christmas time, and I could feel the love that existed between my father and his sister as they laughed and joked with each other. It was only here that he really seemed to relax and could be the man I had once known.

The four of us kids slept in one big quilt-covered bed on the screened-in sleeping porch, boys at the bottom, girls at the top. The only bathroom was outside and called an outhouse. During the day I was OK to go out there and enjoyed reading the Sears catalogue hanging on the wall, which was used in lieu of toilet paper. A little slick but it got the job done. At night it was like entering the Black Lagoon, dark and forbidding and made even more terrifying by my cousins telling me there was a water moccasin living there, and it might just coil right up and bite me on the ass.

It could get pretty cold out there in the backwoods, and the only heat in the cozy house came from the fireplace. Every morning we kids jumped out of the springy bed and ran to stand in front of the roaring pine-scented fire. Once we got our tushies warm Aunt Gladys would give us a big cup of café au lait which was half-strong chicory coffee and sweet milk. If I close my eyes, I can still taste the sweet and sour chestnut flavor of it, a forbidden treat since I wasn't allowed coffee at home.

I loved going to see Uncle Clifford and Aunt Rowena. She was the most gifted seamstress and could just look at a picture of a Dior dress in *Vogue*, cut out a pattern and whip up an identical version of the original. Their three kids, Herbie,

Little Gale and Eddie were sweet, and I enjoyed being with such a loving family.

When September came, I was put back on the train for the return trip and back to my real family who hadn't seemed to notice I had been away at all.

With every family I stayed with, I pretended that they were my real family. I felt safe…no one threatened me, and I was only treated with kindness and love. I was free to be happy. I could even have fun, which while not entirely missing in my life with my parents, was in short supply. It was such joy to live out those wonderful summer days with no fear. I never once saw any of my uncles hit one of their kids. There were reprimands but never whippings. I saw the way families interacted and had real conversations. Maybe they knew the kind of life I led with my parents, but no one ever said anything that I remember. I always dreaded going back home when the summer was over to return to my real family, but the memories were there to comfort me in my loneliness.

Uncle Everett was my father's favorite brother. They were almost like twins as Everett was born only 10 months after my father. It became my father's duty to take care of Everett and till the end of his life he devoted himself to Everett's well-being. The family referred to Everett as a "bachelor man," but Everett was definitely gay. When he was a child, my father, as part of his duty to his brother, had to make sure that Everett wasn't wearing his sister's dress to school. Uncle Everett was a kind and gentle soul and when he came to visit there was laughter and love for a while. One time on a visit, I had taken it upon my 10-year-old self to answer an ad in the newspaper looking for talented boys and girls to be in a new "Our Gang" film. A time and place was scheduled but neither my mother nor my father were the least bit interested in furthering my dream of being a famous actress. Uncle Everett appeared on leave from the Navy just in time to take me to the contest. All the other children, vastly talented, were dressed in dance clothes, tutus and tights or frilly dresses. I had a plain dress, usual oxfords, long braids and no discernible talent. When my turn came, I calmly walked to the center of the stage and recited a poem. Lo and behold I was chosen for a small part. Uncle Everett was as excited as I and promised to come back when the filming started. True to his word, when the day I was to shoot occurred, he arrived in a flurry of excitement and took me to the park where the film crew had set up. I had been told to wear the same dress, oxfords and braids in which I had auditioned. When I arrived and found the assistant to the assistant, I was elated to find I had dialogue!

Scene: Exterior…Park…sidewalk

Action: Kidnappers looking for child star…stop and ask which way she went.

Character: Me

Dialogue: She (pointing wrong way) went thataway!

Well, Uncle Everett and I thought it was wonderful and surely, I would be discovered. Didn't happen and when the completed film was shown no one was available to take me so I never got to see my first screen role.

STEVE

The summer I turned ten, Daddy brought home a stallion that he had purchased from "some good old boy," he said, who was going to sell the horse for horsemeat. My father named him Steve. My father was not a horseman or even close to it. I think the closest he got to a horse was the mule Uncle Everett and he used to plow the field when they were kids.

Steve was the most beautiful animal I had ever seen. He was about sixteen hands tall, black, and sleek shiny coated with a white starred nose. After a few days, Daddy got the newly purchased blanket and saddle from the tack house but, when he tried to put it on, Steve bucked and sent the whole shebang to the ground. He had Mr. Smith, our handyman, hold the horse while he finally got the saddle on. When he was able to mount, with Mr. Smith's help, Steve started to buck but Daddy was ready. He dug his spurs into Steve, making the high-spirited horse rear up and throw Daddy on the ground. My father was not a patient man and meant to have his way with this horse just as he did with people. He got a two-by-four piece of wood, got back in the saddle and when Steve started to buck hit the poor thing right slap dab across his beautiful head. Daddy started trying to lead the now-befuddled horse around the yard. Since he had no idea how to use his knees and reins properly, he devised a method whereby when he wanted Steve to turn right, he would hit him on the left side of his head, and when he wanted to go left the board would be applied to the right side of his head. Steve soon learned to go right and left but the whites of his eyes and the foam from his mouth moved me to tears. I was warned not to go near Steve as he was dangerous, but I often sneaked out of the house just to talk to him, as I understood all too well the misery he withstood.

With the war on, my parents started inviting soldiers from Camp Walters to come on Sundays for barbeque. They would invite their friends, and all would sit in a circle of folding chairs around the one tree in our yard. A big old tomcat, part of the twelve that resided in and around the plant, always came around for these occasions to pounce on a few droppings of beef. One such Sunday, a new friend of my mother's came with her husband for the festivities. She was wearing a pair of black-market nylons, which she proudly showed to my mother. The cat must have noticed as well, as out of the corner of my eye I saw him go into his attack mode. Crouching low to the ground, he crept up close to the woman and then, without warning, threw himself onto her swinging leg, leaving clawed nylons and equally clawed leg before my father chased him up the tree with a handy broom. I don't think she ever came to the house again. The cat lived a long time.

It was on one of those Sundays that a miracle happened when Joe came. He was a very good-looking young soldier who oozed sex appeal, and my mother and I were goners. I was a gawky ten-year-old with long braids and the ever-present oxfords, and he was a knight in shining Army fatigues. His ambition was to be in show business, and he had produced several shows at the camp that were well received. He started coming every Sunday and I practically threw myself at him as soon as he walked in the door. I jumped in his lap and hung on his every utterance like a love-sick cow. The attention, patience and love he showed me were overwhelming, and he must have seen in both my mother and me the loneliness and acute unhappiness that pervaded the house. I so desperately wished that he was my father that I actually asked him to adopt me. I'm sure he was astounded by this request, but after a slight hesitation he agreed. I found a nice piece of paper and a pen, and he wrote, "I Joe Simon, being of sound mind and body do hereby adopt Patricia Ann Crowder to be my daughter as long as we both shall live." He signed it with a flourish, and then I signed, and he dated it June 10, 1944. It was a kind and loving gesture, and one that I wished over and over again was true. I still have that piece of paper, now wrinkled and stained, all these years later.

I believe my mother actually fell in love with him as later in life she said she wished that she had run off with him. Whether or not he returned her ardor, I have no way of knowing but if it were true, we both certainly would have had much different lives, filled with love and laughter instead of fear and tears.

The end of our romance came when one day Joe ventured out from his usual place in our backyard to the stable where he saw Steve.

"Say Mr. Crowder, that's a beautiful stallion you've got there."

"Yes," said Dad, eyeing Joe. "But he's a killer. Takes a firm hand."

"Would you mind if I tried to ride him?" Joe asked. My father, not wanting to be impolite to a man fighting for our country, agreed. He brought Steve out from the corral all white-eyed and skittery, saddled him while Steve was kicking and tossing his head and handed the reins to Joe.

My father looked at Joe and said, "Now, Joe, I warned you about this horse, so don't blame me when he puts you on your ass!"

Joe took the reins, loosened the cinch a little as best he could with Steve snorting and kicking. He stood there for a few minutes waiting for Steve to calm down and mounted as soon as it was safe. We all stood there waiting for the Wild West show. Joe sat quietly for a moment, leaned over and patted Steve on his neck, whispered something in Steve's twitching ear and gently, ever so gently, guided Steve docilely around the open field that lay between the plant and the house. He put Steve through every pace. They trotted, walked, galloped, sidestepped and backed up. That horse looked like Trigger.

Open-mouthed gapes watched until my father yelled, "Hey, you, soldier boy, you showed off enough. Get your ass off my horse!" Joe, nodded at my Father, slowly dismounted, patted Steve's flank while Steve gratefully muzzled him and led him back to the corral.

Joe was never invited back and shortly after that my father shot Steve, saying he had thrown a shoe, developed hoof and mouth disease and had to be destroyed.

SOME FORM OF JUSTICE

The beatings continued on and on unabated. Where was my mother? Didn't she hear me crying until I no longer cried? Was she indifferent to my pain or was she afraid of my father as well? Did he beat her? I never saw him hit her, but the arguments were so loud that I would run out of the house to hide my fear in Shep's loving fur. The aberrant thing was that he was the one who took care of me when I was sick, drove me to school, tried to help me with my homework. I think he considered it to be his duty and responsibility since Mother wouldn't or couldn't care for me. It was certainly hard for me to reconcile that dutiful father with the monster.

One day when I evidently didn't set the table properly, or maybe I sassed him, he slammed my head into a kitchen cabinet right in front of her. She never said a word. The worst occurred when I was twelve. Father and I had been riding, or rather Billy and I were walking, and Father was riding and by the time we got home it was late and I was tired. After three attempts to get my heavy saddle on the hook, him yelling at me all the while, I finally just lay the saddle down on the floor and started for the house. Enraged, he took the cat o' nine tails, a whip with nine knotted tails, and beat me with it until I escaped and ran screaming into the house, nine trails of blood running down my back. My mother, busy making dinner, took one look at me and ran to the door where he was coming after me. She stopped him, saying, "That's enough, Jennings...no more!" He stopped, sank into a kitchen chair.

After a while, he looked up at her and said, "All right...all right, but you just watch, she'll become a juvenile delinquent or worse." He got up, went into the bedroom and shut the door. I don't know why she had been silent all those years, nor do I know why she ended her silence. This was the only time he had drawn blood and I believe she was worried that I would tell someone. Things that went on in the house, stayed in the house. The face we put on in public was of utmost importance, and I wouldn't have dared tell anyone what I endured. I never even thought of running away for fear that the punishment would be greater than the act itself.

What I do know, for sure, is that she wasn't worried about or for me. She didn't take me in her arms and soothe me. If only she could have, just that once, shown me some affection, it would have meant the world to me.

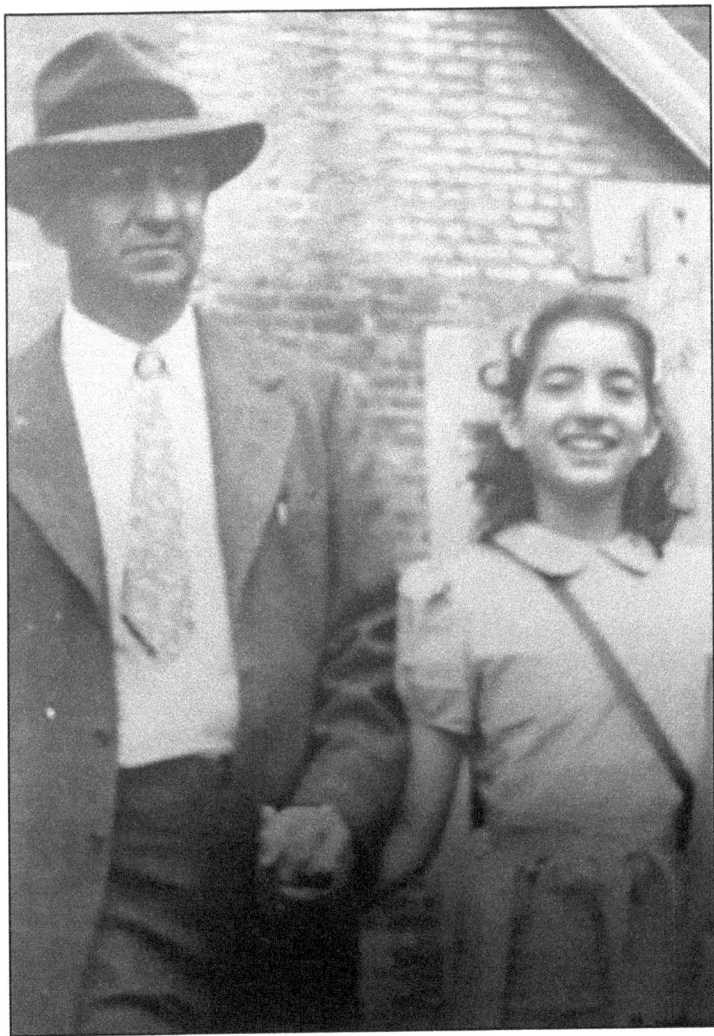

CHANGE
1946-1952

When I was in the middle of the sixth grade Mother was determined that I should go to a better school, so I was transferred to another school with a "better class of people." Boy was she wrong. At Diamond Hill the immigrant parents were doing their best to become good citizens and although they were poor, they taught their children good values, kindness and to be proud of who they were. The new school was made up of a clique of very snobbish and boorish hicks. They hated me on sight, and though I tried to make friends, they already had their friends and there was no room for me.

The junior high was somewhat better because of the music teacher, Miss Winston. She was what was called a "spinster lady" and was laughed at by some of the other teachers but to me she was a Godsend. She was very tall and skinny, had long fingers, wore glasses that were always sliding down her aquiline nose. She had beautiful red hair that she wore in a bun. She spent every chance she could in New York City; a very foreign place where danger lurked on every corner and liberals roamed the streets with the bohemians. She loved to tell us stories of all the latest Broadway shows and sing hits from them. One in particular was "The Saga of Jenny" from *Lady in the Dark*, which was a very sophisticated and dark ditty...way over our heads:

127

Jenny made her mind up at seventy-five
that she would live to be the oldest woman alive
but Gin and Rum and destiny play funny tricks
and poor Jenny kicked the bucket at seventy-six.

The other kids were all bored, but I loved every minute of her class.

My mother, in trying to educate herself in the finer things, had given me a set of books on popular operas and the records that went with them. I fell in love with *Carmen* and memorized the entire book and music. I actually made-up gibberish to the music and acted out the entire libretto, playing Carmen, Don Jose and the other characters. When Miss Winston heard of this unusual gift, she asked me to perform *Carmen* for the music class. Well, she loved my performance, but the kids were ruthless in their derision, so that was the end of my one-girl opera career.

In high school I was a member of the Drama Club headed by a wonderful and pragmatic teacher, Mrs. Putman. I only remember seeing her in the same dark grey dress every day, wearing sensible shoes. She had a gift to bring out the best in the small cadre of creative misfits who took drama. Although most of us were "D" students, we were probably the smartest kids in the mostly redneck and ignorant setting in which we found ourselves. For the first time since I left the security of the Diamond Hill school, I felt accepted. There was no judgement. We all worked together as an ensemble to put on a play in which we all, no matter how we looked or sounded, got to perform and be stars for a night or two. It was thrilling to be up there on stage in front of a mostly receptive audience. I always played the goofy girl or ugly best friend, who always got the laughs if not the boy. I had wanted to be an actress since I saw *Gone with the Wind*, and the Drama Club only made that desire stronger. I loved taking on the persona of another person. I could escape the unhappiness of my own life by living, for a while, in another world altogether, a world where there was love and joy, not pain and misery. It was the one place where I got approval. When I was on that stage and people were laughing I was in heaven. There is no better feeling in the world than to experience the love that comes over the footlights when you're in the groove and at one with the audience.

Unfortunately, my parents never attended any of the performances in which I appeared, and in later life when I had a career, I would tell Mom when one of my appearances would be shown on TV. When I would call her later to get her reaction. She said, "Oh, I didn't see it. I must have fallen asleep." At the age of one hundred and two, she said, "You did some acting, didn't you?" What? "Yes, Mother," I murmured. "Do you have a scrapbook or something?" Oh my God! "Yes Mother," I said. We looked at my life as an actress, while she seemed truly interested and every now and then, "Oh, I didn't know you were in that." It felt so good to finally be recognized but also a little sad that it had taken so long.

I decided that I would major in drama in college with the goal of becoming a famous Broadway star. My parents, realizing that I was probably too dumb, based on my grades, to major in anything else, and hoping I would get married instead, went along with my decision.

Other than the drama department, school was boring, and the dean constantly told my parents that I just wasn't working up to my potential. I didn't know exactly what my potential was and really didn't care.

I had been a cute little girl, but that changed as I entered my teens. I wore thick glasses, had braces on my teeth and, seemingly overnight, had grown a very large nose that earned me the detested nickname of Beaky. I did have a lovely figure, but my face overshadowed it. I was miserable. There were boys I liked but the feeling wasn't returned. I had several girl-friends that understood, and I developed a small group of other so-called oddballs and misfits to hang out with. It was a pretty rough school. There were always some fifteen and six-teen-year-old girls who already looked like the women they would become hanging out in the girls bathroom where they exchanged some red colored pills. My all-knowing friend, Marion, told me they were drugs that made them feel like they were drunk. That made perfect sense since I had gotten drunk, or, at least I thought I was drunk, one New Year's Eve on champagne that my mother's best friend gave me. She made me promise not to tell anyone and said, "Every girl should learn how to drink champagne so when you go out on a date, you'll know what to order." I thought that was very good advice and have tried to adhere to that philosophy as often as possible.

The boys they hung out with were called the Golden Chain Gang. During and after the Friday night ritual football games, the GCG would gang up on kids from the other schools under the stands and beat the shit out of them just for kicks. I tried to stay away from these miscreants, but God forgive you if you got in their way. One of the "Dolls" as they called themselves, really had it in for me for some unknown reason. She was a guard on the junior basketball team, the only sport in which I was halfway decent, and at every practice she would push, shove, and slam my body so hard that I would limp home covered with bruises. I approached her in the shower room, "Hey, Jean Ann, did I do something to you? Maybe you could stop hitting me so hard. It's just practice, you know." She was a tough little sucker, all bunched-up muscles and caved-in stomach.

"You wanna meet me outside after school today?" she barked. I tried to move away, but she grabbed me. "You're scared, ain't ya?" she snarled, sharp little teeth snapping like castanets. Yeah, I was scared. I didn't know how to fight, and I wasn't eager to learn.

"You just leave me alone," I said as I pried myself loose. "I don't know what you think I've done, but whatever it is I'm sorry." She turned away with a grunt. I was very careful after that to stay as far away from her or any of the other "Dolls."

THE HAY HOUSE

One day Bobby, a boy that I knew slightly, asked if he and two other boys could come out to look at the horses. I was thrilled. Maybe Bobby liked me. He was very cute in a hayseed sort of way. He and the other two arrived, and I introduced them to my Mother and took them out to the barn. One of the boys, sitting up on the railing of the stable asked, "Hey, girl. Are you on the rag?"

I had absolutely no idea what he was talking about and said so, but they just looked at one another exchanging winks. Soon, one of the boys asked, "What are those little houses out there?" pointing at the small house behind the stables that were used for various things.

"Oh, just stuff, you know saddles in one and another has hay," I said.

"Hay, huh," said the big one with the buzz cut hair. "How about you show us that hay house."

"Sure," I said, "Come on." We walked toward the hay house and as soon as I opened the door, and Bobby and I walked in, the other two boys slammed the door and latched it. Bobby threw me down on the hay, got on top of me and squirmed all around. "What are you doing," I yelled. "Get off me!" I pushed him off and screamed so loud that the boys unlatched the door, and I ran out and into our house yelling for my mother. It was a terrible experience and although nothing really happened, I felt like I had been raped, and the whole incident really scared me. Bobby, of course told the other boys that he had been successful in his attempt, and they left laughing and patting him on the back. I told my mother and when my father came home, she told him what had happened. Over my protestations, they decided that Bobby's parents should be told. I just wanted to forget the whole thing, but if my reputation was on the line, that meant theirs was also and God forbid that it get around that they had raised a round-heeled girl. We got in the car and drove to Bobby's house where my parents confronted Bobby's parents who were horrified.

Bobby was called out of his room and his father said, "Son, I'm hearing something real bad about your behavior toward this young girl here. I want to know if it's true or not."

Bobby looked at me and hung his head. "Sam and Petey set it all up. I didn't do nothing and I'm just real sorry." His confession did actually make me feel better, but as I feared, the story had spread throughout the whole school, and I was considered an "easy lay" until the day I graduated. When I got a call for a date, the first such call I had ever had, I was excited but soon realized that the boy was only after one thing. Every time I walked down the hall or the aisle of a classroom some of the boys would make crude gestures. It was humiliating and my self-esteem sank even lower than it already was.

I started hanging out with a new group of kids. Doris "C for Chesty" and I became fast friends. She was quite advanced in many ways for her age, and I'd go with her to the drive-in where she'd meet one of the older boys who hung out there.

She and the boy would make out while I sat in the back, drinking a beer or two the boy brought while trying to watch the movie. We played hooky at least twice a week, and my grades plummeted even lower than they had been. The strange thing was that my parents saw that I was failing and that I went out with Doris a lot, but they never questioned what might be going on in my life.

When I was 17, I had an attack of appendicitis and had it removed. The rumor at school was that I had had an abortion. I did the smart thing and kept that rumor to myself. They probably would have made the doctor go to the school and make an announcement of my innocence over the loudspeaker. I actually remained a virgin until I was nineteen.

I did have one boyfriend in high school. His name was Tommy, and he was very sweet and actually liked me for who I was. We went to the senior prom and when I had my appendix out, he brought me flowers, but I wasn't interested in a boy that liked me. I wanted the boy I could never have. I often rejected a boy or man who was kind, decent and really cared for me for an impossible guy who didn't give a flying fuck about me. Again, I believe this pattern stemmed from the fact that while hating the monster, I was also desirous of the monster's love. No wonder I was so fucked up.

MOTHER'S MALADY

On and off mother had suffered from a mysterious malady for which none of the doctors she went to over the years could find a remedy. Every time the ailment became unbearable, she took to her bed, writhing in agony. As these episodes became more frequent my father even took her to the Mayo clinic, and finally, she was told that it was all in her mind, a general cop-out in those days if there was no evident disease. There was one last chance. A famous surgeon who had operated on Dwight Eisenhower was in Galveston for a series of lectures, and they were able to get an appointment with this esteemed man. The night before she was to see him, as she bent over the motel bathtub to turn on the faucet, she collapsed. Father rushed her to the hospital where it was determined that her intestines had burst. The famous surgeon was called and performed emergency surgery during which he removed three feet of her colon and joined the large colon to the small, a very radical procedure that he had only done one other time. I was told my mother probably wouldn't survive, and I was put on the train to Galveston to say goodbye.

When I walked into the hospital room, she lay with tubes running into and out of every part of her body. The room smelled like I imagined death would smell. It was scary seeing her like that so pale and helpless. The woman who churned her own butter, washed the sheets in the sink and dried them on the clothesline, who cooked three meals a day including dessert every night and kept the house spotless was a rag doll in a sea of blood, dark yellow urine and pus collecting drip by drip in bottles hanging from the bed. I saw my father kneeling beside the bed holding her hand, "Thelma," he begged. "Just come back to me. I'll change. I promise I'll be a better husband…." He droned on and on. I didn't know what to do, I thought I should do something…kiss her or hold her hand or something but I was frozen in fear and felt like I was going to be sick with the horrible smell and the stuff coming out of her. I felt no sadness. There were no tears, no sad feelings, just gut-wrenching fear, and I don't know if the fear was for her or for me. I sat across the room. Nobody paid me any attention at all which was fine with me. After a while they ushered me out of the room, while they were working on her, trying to save her life. I guess my father and I stayed in a motel in Galveston and went every day to see her, but I have absolutely no memory of that time after the initial visit at all. The next thing I remember was that she was all well and having the time of her life, but it must have been months.

She later told me that she had had an out of the body experience and that she actually was on the ceiling in the corner of the room watching everything. She saw me come into the room and my father on his knees begging and the doctor shaking his head over and over. She wanted to leave but couldn't. She said that suddenly she was back in her body and opened her eyes. It was an amazing recovery, and to celebrate, my father bought her a brand-new Buick.

REBEL WITH A CAUSE

While my parents were out almost every night having a good time with their friends after she got well, I got a bright idea of how, while they were out, I could have a little fun instead of being stuck at home. I called Doris, "Can you get the car? Come get me!"

She came over, "What's going on?" she asked.

I just showed her where my mother kept the keys to the brand-new Buick, the love of her new life. "I'm going to get a copy of the key and while they're gone, we can run around and have fun," I said. I also got the keys to the front gate and the house. Doris was all for it so we went off to the key smith who, fortunately, didn't question me too closely when I told him my mother had sent me.

The next time my parents went out I put the phone off the hook, got in the beautiful slate blue car, locked the gate behind me, picked up Doris and went to the Malt Shop where everyone hung out. When they saw me driving that brand-new Buick, I was instantly popular. Five or six kids piled in the car and we just drove around for a while, yelling out the windows and Hal, who hadn't known I existed before then, actually pulled down his pants and mooned some old lady. Finally, it was time to go home before my parents came back, promising to come back when I could get the car again. All was well when I got home. I put the car back exactly as she had left it, unlocked the house and fell into bed elated and thrilled.

A couple of nights later, after my parents left, I picked Doris up and off we went joyriding all over town creating teenage havoc and ruckus. This went on for a few weeks until one of the kids suggested that we go up on the road around Lake Worth where some of the kids from other schools met to play Chicken. That sounded like a fine idea, having absolutely no idea how the game was played. We drove up to the lake, parked and waited. Soon, a couple of other cars came by filled with kids with the sole purpose of trying to kill themselves. Doris and I watched for a while and then arranged with another group of stupid kids to "Play Chicken" which consisted of driving at full speed directly toward one another until one turned Chicken and pulled over. This, by the way, was four years before *Rebel Without a Cause* caused such uproar. It was a very dangerous game at which I found I excelled. I seemed to have nerves of steel and one by one all the other cars pulled over with me the winner. Some winner, but hey I was popular for the first time in my life and I basked in that glow. That being popular by those standards wasn't desired by most sane people didn't enter my mind.

One night the fun and the danger came to a very abrupt end when arriving home, I found the property surrounded by cops. My parents had returned home earlier than expected, and finding me and the car gone, thought I had been kidnapped! They were seemingly so glad to see me that I wasn't even disciplined. I actually felt that I should have had some kind of punishment. To get away free and clear from such a really dangerous escapade only led me to believe that I could do whatever I wanted without any consequences.

TESSIE
1952-1953

I finally graduated from high school with mostly C's and D's. The only good grades I ever made were from Drama and Music. I actually was pretty good at typing, a skill that saved my ass on many an occasion when looking for a job.

It was time to find a college and that would prove difficult. I wanted to go to the University of Texas to study Theatre, but I couldn't get in with such miserable grades. In fact, the only school that would take me was Texas State College for Women, an all women university, not known for its Theatre Department, but I wanted to leave home so badly I would have gone to Hell just to get away.

"Tessie" as TSCW was fondly referred to by the staff and students had a very fine reputation for physical education, not Theatre or, as they called it, Drama but as I had little or no choice, I was determined to make the best of what was available. There was a pretty good radio department where I learned how to spin a record and to segue from one record to the next. There were two turntables in the booth next to one another and it took some skill to pick up the needle from one and have the other ready to go smoothly. It was a challenge and one of the few things I enjoyed at Tessie. The drama department was small and since there were no boys, the taller girls had to play the men's' roles, so I never got to be a "girl" the entire year.

Most of the women were at Tessie for a degree in P.E. so they could teach or further their skills as professionals in their chosen field, and although not all the women who majored in P.E. were gay, there were certainly many students and teachers who were very masculine in appearance.

A few days after I arrived, I was walking on the quad when a very handsome, tall blond-haired boy in tight jeans and a plaid shirt stopped me. "Hi" he said. "My name's Charlie. Are you new?"

"Yeah," I swooned, "I'm a freshman."

"You wanna go have a soda," he asked. Gosh, I thought, maybe he was the brother of one of the girls, so I accepted his invitation, thrilled to have such a good-looking boy take notice of me let alone take me for a soda. We walked across the campus and into a drugstore near the junior and senior dorms. When we walked in at least ten very masculine-looking women started hooting, hollering and patting Charlie on the back. Oh my God, I finally realized that Charlie was a girl! Evidently there was a bet on which of the butch women would be the first to get a "Frosh." I had never even seen a lesbian let alone ten of them in one place. I hightailed it out of there and back to relatively safe territory a trail of laughter following me.

It really was an amazing place. On special occasions our dorm mother, Mrs. Loomis, stood in the middle of the lobby atrium while we hung over the second-floor balcony singing "Beautiful, Beautiful Brown Eyes" to her. I never knew how this started or why, but I still can't hear that song without thinking of the large brown-eyed woman who ran our dorm like an army barracks.

I was able to make some good friends at Tessie, and Jeannie, my very best friend and I are still close. She was a very beautiful young woman, tall, with a regal bearing and a lovely face. She had beautiful hands that were long and expressive. She could tell a whole story just with her hands, long fingers with their always brightly painted nails waving in the air, a cigarette dangling from the fingertips. We were part of a group of girls who liked to get in trouble. One of the girls had a car and after "lights out," at 10, we would meet at the back door of the dorm and sneak out, leaving a small wooden wedge in the door opening so we could get back in later and take off for Lake Dallas to drink beer and have a good time. We met some Chicano boys once while on the loose and started hanging out with them. They called themselves "Pachucos," but I don't think they were gang affiliated. They wore zoot suits, styled their hair in ducktails and liked to strut. They were very sweet boys and were always perfect gentlemen. We were never caught during the course of our innocent meanderings, all the more surprising due to the diligence of Brown Eyes.

While we were attending summer school, due to our dismal grades, Jeannie and I decided to talk our folks into letting us go to another college together. We just barely amassed enough good grades to get into Texas Christian University in Fort Worth, a somewhat step up from Tessie, and the best part was that there were boys there.

I was not too keen on having to live at home while going to school, but over the summer my father was given a huge promotion and was sent back to Houston to oversee the business as one of the vice presidents. Hooray! I could live in the dorm.

TCU

1953

TCU was the home of the famed football team, the Horned Toads (more appropriately called the horny toads). Jeannie was my roommate and instead of being thrilled to be away from "Tessie," we were both miserable in this temple to testosterone. The drama department was run by a very strange and pedantic German who only liked to critique scenes and didn't seem to be interested in actually producing a play. "Vat are ya do'ink Miss Croooder? Ya don't sprechen the English, ya?"

Most of the students were from West Texas and Jeannie and I thought the bulk of them were just rednecks and boorish. I never had a real date the whole time I was there except for once when Alta, the nympho who lived across the hall, asked us if we were willing to go out with two guys of her acquaintance on a blind date? Being a Saturday and desperate we agreed. The time approached, and we were all decked out in our best "going to a nice place for dinner" duds. When the boys arrived, we were mortified to discover that they were really blind! They had another friend drive us to a juke joint out on Highway 59 where we had beers served on an oilcloth-covered table adorned with sardine cans for ashtrays. The jukebox blared out country and western, and we danced with them as best we could under the circumstances. They were really nice young men, well dressed, hair combed carefully, shoes polished and shamefully, we were not very kind to them. We pleaded headaches so we could leave early. They walked us back to the dorm, and we said a hurried good night. I only hope that they found some lovely girls who cared for them. They must have been terribly lonely in the atmosphere of the 50s.

Alta said, "Well, you said you were desperate!" She was a case. As a self-acclaimed nymphomaniac, she bragged that she had keys from every motel in Fort Worth and put them up on a pegboard to prove it. One night I wandered into her room to borrow something or other only to discover her sitting up in bed chewing on her toenails.

I did everything I could to try to gain the attention I so desperately needed. I cut my hair very short and wore long flowing skirts and peasant blouses, unlike the preppy and sweet attire all the other girls wore. Jeannie and I made a point of standing out in the sea of rednecks where we were considered weird and for good reason. There was a social area with a jukebox near the cafeteria where we could play soul, or "N–ger" music, as the rednecks called it and do the dirty bop until someone would change to the more acceptable Bob Willis and the Texas Playboys. We once drank most of the football team under the table. I got no pleasure from these antics and only deepened my feelings of inadequacy. I did make some friends from the drama department and the ballet kids who, when they weren't rehearsing, were fun. Most of the ballet guys were gay, trying desperately to appear straight so as not to be beaten up by the homophobic assholes that permeated the campus.

Every year during the Fort Worth Fat Stock Show and Rodeo, a weeklong hoot and holler tribute to the Ole West where men were men and women were either virgins or whores, TCU participated in this tribute by everyone wearing western attire and participating in a number of events. The Ugliest Man on Campus was one such event and the year I was there a woman proudly won it. There was also a talent show put on by the kids from ballet and drama. I chose to sing "Pistol Packing Mama" and was booed off the stage most likely due to the fact that I couldn't sing.

To say my life was miserable would be a gross understatement. To escape this tortured existence, I walked as often as I could to the nearby Fort Worth Zoo.

I have always liked the big cats best and I particularly like the panthers. There was one who was huge, shiny, black, sleek with muscles meant to spring at a moment's notice reduced to pacing back and forth in his tiny eight by twelve cage. Every time I entered the zoo, I went directly to his cage as if drawn by a magnet. I began to talk to him. I told him how beautiful he was, how miserable I was and how happy he made me feel just looking at him. After several weeks of visiting, he stopped pacing, looked me right in the eye with his great yellow pools. Mine wide and a little frightened. I stood absolutely still and then he came close to the bars and began rubbing his flank against the rails. There was only a small hedge between the cage and the sidewalk, and it was actually possible to stick one's hands through the bars. With no thought of any consequence, I reached through and began stroking his bristly flank. He moved closer and I continued until he moved away, and I carefully removed my hand. This went on for several weeks until one day he turned toward me and began rubbing his head against the bars. I reached in and began scratching his ear. He did not stop rubbing and actually leaned into my hand. Then, from deep within his body came a throbbing low sound, gaining in strength and intensity the more I scratched. He was purring. It sent chills throughout my entire being to feel that I was one with this magnificent creature. I slowly removed my hand and backed away as I had a class to attend. He looked at me as though to say, "All right, you can go now." From then on, every time I went to see him there was an unspoken agreement between us that I was meant to pet him. Sometimes he pressed his flank and at other times his head but at no time was there the slightest hint of aggression. Only love existed between us. He seemed to know when I entered the park and would come immediately to me as soon as he saw me. I realize now that I had more in common with the panther than I knew then. He and I shared the misery of being trapped. He in a cage and I locked in my inner turmoil from which there seemed no escape.

Finally, the school year came to an end and I was able to persuade my parents to allow me to transfer to yet another university far away from Cow Town. On the last day I was able to visit my friend, I spent a long time telling him how very much he meant to me, that I loved him but that I would never see him again. He put his paw out as though to stop me, then pulled it back in. I took one last look at him as I slowly walked away, tears sliding down my face.

HOUSTON
1953-1954

Jeannie and I parted ways at the end of the school year both vowing to keep in touch. She was going to finish her education at a school near where she lived in East Texas. I thought that was probably the end of our friendship since I was going to go to New York to become a famous actress and would never see her again. Little did I know that we would actually become roommates again when she had graduated with a degree in Special Education and had gotten a job teaching in Houston and I had come back from adventures in San Francisco to work at the Alley Theatre on my first real step toward the greatness that was sure to come.

In the summer of 1953, amazingly, my parents agreed to let me have plastic surgery. Mother, I believe, was acutely aware that I was no prize package and hard to market, and she talked my father into having the hated beak remodeled. So, with glasses gone, braces removed, and my new Elizabeth Taylor nose I was ready to take on the world. It really was a remarkable change and for the first time I was considered pretty. But, even after the surgery I couldn't accept the fact that I was actually a very beautiful young woman. I had widow-peaked blue-black hair, beautiful hazel eyes, green rimmed and a really knock-out figure and new nose, but still I carried that image of ugly girl/woman for many years.

I was able to transfer my credits to the University of Houston. What a difference! The U of H was like heaven. It was everything I had hoped college would be. I was asked to join a sorority but soon found that there was so much activity in the drama department that I had no time for silly sorority rites.

A terrific woman, Lela Blount, a gifted teacher and director, ran the drama department. The head of stagecraft was an interesting man who kept a chimpanzee in a large cage in the living room of his and his wife's small apartment. The chimp wore diapers and was treated like a baby by the two of them. I was terrified when invited over that the chimp would get out of his cage and go on some sort of rampage, wrecking everything and creating general havoc.

We were encouraged by Lela to gain some knowledge of The Theatre by hanging out on weekends at one of the small theatres in the city. I started as an apprentice at The Alley, an area Theatre that had an excellent reputation, jobbing in big stars to play the leads in some of the productions. I started on door C of the arena stage. My job was to be sure the door was closed when the actor made his or her entrance. After proving myself proficient at that job, I was soon assigned to help with the wardrobe changes that, in some cases, were lighting fast. I was thrilled to be around real actors and watched their every move as much as I could and the director, Nina Vance, was encouraging.

At the university I was cast as Anitra, the dancing girl in *Peer Gynt*. I had a wonderful time with the department's best actor, Maury Kennelly playing the lead. It was thrilling watching him perform. I have seen few actors before or since who so imbued themselves in a role as he did. Unfortunately, he was too sensitive to expose himself to rejection and the stress of looking for a job, so he went back to Steubenville, Ohio and, as far as I know, lived the rest of his life there without ever treading the boards again.

The best role I had while there was as Lady Macduff in "The Scottish Play." Maury played the lead again, marvelous and commanding. While at The Alley I met a young actor, Ernesto, a man whom I liked immediately. He was a good actor and very encouraging to me. He helped me learn to speak the beautiful language of Shakespeare and taught me how to carry myself and to use my own qualities and instincts to actually try to become, not act but become, the sad and terrified woman who loses so much so tragically. Ernesto stood in the back of the theatre each night that we played to lead the applause at the end of my scene.

We saw each other as much as we could and soon fell in love. One night he made love to me, a nineteen-year-old virgin in the back seat of his old beaten up black jalopy. He didn't use any protection and I didn't know enough to use anything, but I soon got the name of a doctor from my roommate to get a diaphragm, which was an antiquated method of contraception. It was a rubber ring that had to be filled with spermicide then inserted into the vagina in such a way that it would act as a cervical cap to hopefully prevent those pesky little sperms from getting to the eggs. It was very messy and definitely not foolproof.

Ernesto wanted to get married, but my parents certainly

didn't think him suitable marriage material and wanted me to forget about actors, especially Mexican ones, and date someone of a so-called better class.

SEVILLA IN HOUSTON

Ernesto wanted me to meet his family but was worried that I might not approve of them because they were extremely poor. I assured him that would be the farthest thing from my mind so one night he invited me for dinner, and I accepted.

We arrived at the small, modest house where I was greeted at the front door by his mother, a small round woman who welcomed me with an embrace that was all encompassing. Ernesto's father, a large man with green eyes just like Ernesto's, black hair and large callused hands from a lifetime of hard labor greeted me as warmly as Ernesto's mother had. Anita, Ernesto's sister, an exotic dancer by trade, had the gypsy strain of her Seville ancestors evident in her beauty and bearing. We ate beans and rice made with love and mysterious spices that were delicious. I had never felt so at home anywhere. After dinner there was entertainment. The father pulled out a guitar and began playing a soft flamenco that gained in intensity until the mother began to sing a haunting refrain, and then Anita began to dance, her feet pounding the floor with authority, her castanets clicking in rhythm. Ernesto picked up two spoons and held them between his fingers in such a way that they instantly became musical instruments. As the intensity grew, the whole house shook with such wild abandonment that I felt we would just lift up and fly away. Then it was over.

Ernesto drove me back to my parents' beautiful, antique-filled home, where perfume wafted through the air, but what I had just witnessed showed me that life was not about what you had. Rather, I had experienced true love and beauty in a tiny home on the wrong side of town where the beds had no sheets. It was a valuable lesson that was to serve me well in the years to come.

SAN FRANCISCO
1954-1957

In early 1954 my Father was transferred from Houston to San Francisco to run the company's bone plant, making gelatin from cleaned bones. He had developed a new method of cleaning the bones that left no residue and was considered revolutionary at the time, but the patent belonged to the company and my Father never received a dime for his invention.

Mother was ecstatic. Finally, she would become the person she had always wanted to be, wear the clothes she coveted and live the lifestyle she desired and felt she deserved. I finally realized that she had also fantasized about being Scarlett. She wanted to be that beautiful woman who had lifted herself out of the ruins of her life to become a desirable rich woman. Mother came from living on the floor of a tent to the eighth floor of a Nob Hill apartment building overlooking the San Francisco Bay. She had achieved her life-long dream, and it was here that she was the happiest in her long life.

The two of us even got along better. She always wore Black Narcissus perfume that permeated all her clothes and followed her from room to room, leaving want and desire on my part, I so desperately wanted to be her. To have her beauty, her way with men, her wit and the one thing I was to never have, her love.

I, of course, wanted to stay in Houston and finish school

as I was now in my Junior year, but my parents were afraid that I would run off with Ernesto, so I went with them protesting all the way. I think, had I stayed in Houston, I would have married Ernesto. He was the only man in my life who truly understood me, and I believe I would have been happy but living in San Francisco changed my feelings.

I thought, since I was forced to be there, I could go to Berkeley to finish my studies, but my parents thought that Berkeley was "The Hotbed of Communism," and refused to send me there. In retaliation, I refused to go to any school at all and sat on the couch of our beautiful apartment on Nob Hill for a month until I got so bored with myself that I finally got up and ventured out into the fantastic new world of San Francisco.

It sure as Hell wasn't Texas. I decided that I could be a model, so I found a modeling school called The House of Charm, and with my parents' encouragement signed up for a six-week course that taught one everything one needed to know to become a model. There were all types of girls there: tall, short, fat, and slim. I fit into the tall, slim category so I was singled out after three weeks to actually do a runway show. I had to walk down a raised aisle, pivot just so, one foot in front of the other and sashay back to change into another outfit. A snap! My first show was lingerie modeling. I wore beautiful lace bras and girdles to which gauze skirts were added for modesty's sake. The show was about an hour long and I made a hundred bucks! Bliss! I didn't have to finish the course as I was now a real model and they refunded the remaining money. I continued to do runway modeling for several months and then started getting calls to model for buyers who came to town to see the latest designer clothes. It was very different than doing runway and the pay was much better. You had to change in the small hotel or conference room bathroom and there were always a few guys who wanted to finger you as well as the goods. Hands got slapped politely as God knows most of the girls really needed the job and you didn't want to offend the buyer. No "Me Too" in that day and antiquated age.

Some of the other models and I would go out after work for a drink or two. San Francisco has always been a cosmopolitan city, almost European. There was a degree of sophistication that I certainly had not encountered in Texas. There was a wonderful mixture of culture. The Italians who had settled in the city were in the North Beach area. The Chinese, a huge part of California history, had one of the largest Chinese communities in the country. Then there were the Bluebloods who ran the city and its cultural events and lived on Nob Hill or the younger socialites in the Marina. The working class lived in mixed neighborhoods throughout the city, and last, but definitely not least were the Beats...the poets, musicians, actors, artists who all flocked to the City in this golden age of creative outpouring and decadence. Mother played bridge with and wined and dined some of the new guard if not the old. I had never seen her happier and she was so busy I was pretty much left on my own to do whatever I wanted, which was everything.

Soon, I was sent out on an interview for a suit manufacturer's model. I was the perfect size twelve: 34-24-34. It was probably closer to the new size four in today's tiny size race to perfection. The designer was a well-known manufacturer by the name of David Crystal, a very nice man. He treated me like the daughter he may or may not have had, as I never learned anything of his personal life. It was a really well-paying job, and I enjoyed the joking and camaraderie of the seamstresses and others happily working under his employment.

Ernesto had been looking for work in Los Angeles and came up to see me when my parents went on a two-week trip. We fucked our brains out, then did it all over again. We had a huge fight over some silly thing I don't even remember, and he went back to LA. About that time my wild, adventuresome, impulsive side began to kick in, and I really wanted to be with someone else just to compare notes, you might say.

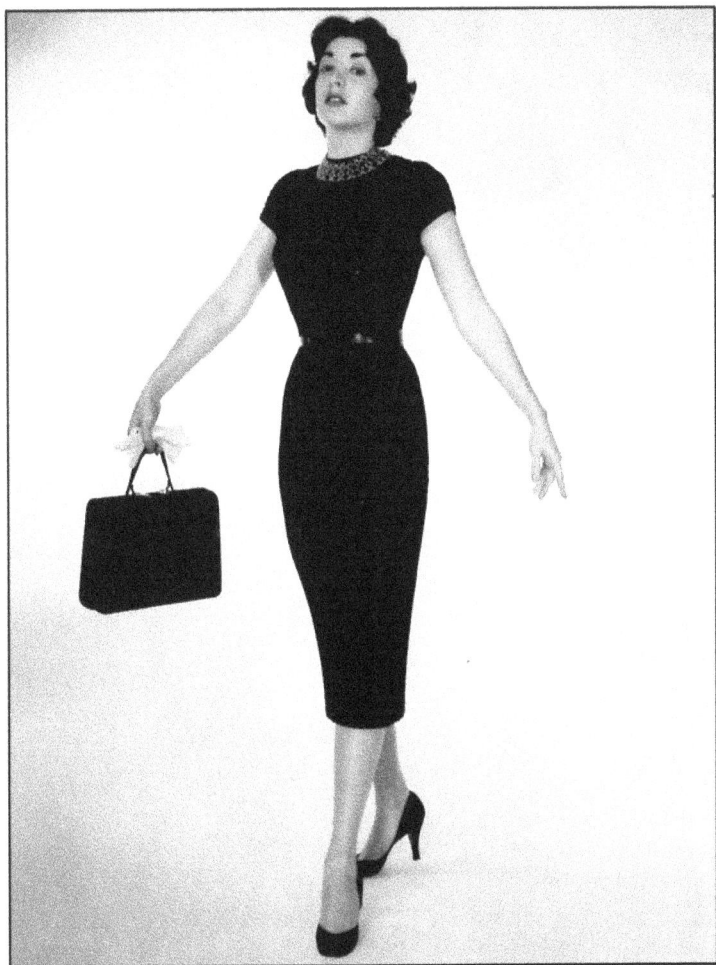

LARRY

The first man I chose for comparison was Larry, a cab driver by trade. I met him in a bar and while he was not at all handsome or desirable in any way I was taken by his vocabulary and seeming knowledge of literature. He was probably at least ten years older than I with long blond scraggly hair, sharp peregrine eyes, and a cigarette dangling from his yellow crooked teeth and nicotine-stained fingers. He claimed to be a writer and I was always a sucker for writers. It never dawned on me that anyone could say they were writers, never having written a word. However, being with him was like living in a Damon Runyon world, exciting and unlike anything in Texas. He lived in a run-down apartment in North Beach, paint peeling off the worn banister leading up to his small but neat lair.

We made love on a mattress that had certainly seen a lot of action and better days. I can't say his lovemaking was much better than Ernesto's just a lot of humping and sweat but at least he wore protection. His fantasy ambition was to be the next Saroyan whom he quoted on a daily basis. "Listen to this," he said. "This is just what I need to get me out of my writer's block." He quoted, "'How do you write? You write man, you write, that's how.' Isn't that genius?" he asked. Yes, wise words but as it turned out, he was much more interested in the ponies than putting pen to paper.

One day he said, "Hey, my Rose, come look at my new

system." He showed me a strange object hanging from a chain. "See, here," he said. "This here object is not only a work of art, but it has great powers of divination." It was indeed beautiful. There were seven crystal gemstones graduated in size down to a point. "Now watch this," he said holding the object in his hand. "This here is a pendulum and now you're gonna be the first to see the miracle of the Pendulum!" He put the racing form on the wobbly, paint-peeled kitchen table and held the pendulum above it. Soon, the pendulum began to swing back and forth across the day's pick of horses until it slowed down and came to rest on one, the winning one. It was pretty amazing. We had to go to Tanforan to test this new winning method.

Tanforan was the thoroughbred-racing track near San Francisco where we spent a lot of afternoons to test his latest method. Unfortunately, this latest system proved to be as totally unreliable as all the others had been.

During the time between April and October of 1942, Tanforan had been used as a Japanese internment camp with approximately seventy-five hundred Bay Area residents confined there. Many were forced to live in the hastily converted grandstands and horse stables. Stalls that had been designed to hold a single thoroughbred filly or stallion were used to house as many as five of our tax paying citizens who lost everything during this shameful era. In strange retribution, Tanforan burned to the ground on July 31st, 1964.

Larry was a kind and gentle person, and I was glad to learn something of the seamier side of life, but he never seemed to have any extra money and I got tired of "loaning" him my hard-earned money to put down on a sure thing and after a couple of weeks decided to move on.

JIM

I met a new prospect in my favorite North Beach watering hole, Vesuvio's Café, a hangout of some of the "Beat" writers of that era. Jack Kerouac, who later wrote *On the Road*, was a regular when he was in town as was Alan Ginsberg. I don't remember whether or not I ever met any of the Beats in person, but I went to many poetry and jazz sessions going on in every back alley in the Beach, and I was a huge fan of Ginsberg. I have a first editon of "Howl" which I bought next door from Vesuvio's at the City Lights Bookstore. I began to fancy myself a poet and began furiously scribbling my bon mots on napkins and coasters, and on the back of drink receipts...

NORTH BEACH

Why must you carry on this endless searching for my soul
Why can't we just laugh and talk and be as un-bohemian as
      we are neurotic
North Beach holds no spell for me – neither do its people
I prefer not to discuss my sexual capabilities, Zen Buddhism,
      Hinduism,
Shinto or take a stand on jazz
And if I should advocate ambition, it's just that I'm sane and
      have not
Learned well the art of sitting

NORTH BEACH II

Cable, tables, knives and forks
Gin and tonic, Aesop's Fables
Collages, mirages
Snow in the jungle, dusk at dawn
Drowned ducks, one broken cup
Dead memories of an indifferent past
Can the perverted Genie cry as he stares through his lopsided
      bubbles
Does he know why I loved you or does he care

I was sitting in my favorite high-backed plantation chair
when I spied a devastatingly handsome man across the room.
He had sandy hair cut short. He was tall and slightly stooped,
which later I attributed to his fatalistic attitude. He wandered
over and squatted down beside me.

"I've been watching you. I would like to paint you," he
said.

Well, that was a new one, but "Yeah, why not," I said. Sitting for an artist was one of the few things I hadn't done yet.
We had a drink, one of the many we were to have, and I
learned that Jim was a painter/depressive who came from a
very wealthy Chicago family to live and paint in North Beach.
His very famous father was a Supreme Court Judge and I
think Jim just wanted to get away from him and all the other
trappings of his past preppy life.

He lived in a crummy hotel that I, of course, adored since

it proved I was living a true bohemian life and with a real painter. The hotel was just across Broadway from The Hungry i., a famous club and bar run by Enrico Banducci. The i was the showcase for many up-and-coming comedians, such as Shelly Berman, Mort Sahl, Lenny Bruce, Nichols & May and many others. I was fortunate to have seen Berman, Sahl and most of all Lenny Bruce with his wicked, profane, profound humor. I didn't realize at the time that these amazing creative people would become the icons of a golden age in comedy and what a gift it was to have been able to see and hear these legends.

We spent most of every evening at one dive or another in North Beach getting drunk on cheap wine and then home to climb the well-worn stairs to his room which consisted of a small iron bed with an unusually ratty mattress, a bedside table and a small four-drawer dresser neither of which would have been accepted at Goodwill. Across the room stood a once-white sink and a couple of frayed towels hanging from a nail. The floors were bare wood, a godsend since who knows what would have nested there. The toilet was down the hall and used by the derelicts that resided there. Even though I had read that you couldn't get anything off a toilet seat, I squatted whenever I absolutely had to go. I guess he really hated the life he had lived in Chicago because this place was the pits. He liked to paint in the morning after we had dragged our hung-over bodies out of bed, across the street for coffee with a shot, and back again. He would throw open the torn shades covering the flyspecked windows, set up the easel and begin to paint.

During these new sexual adventures, I should mention that my parents thought I was spending the nights with my girlfriend Sally who was more than willing to lie for me since she thought I was too virginal, whatever that meant. I think my mother knew what was going on, but she was so busy enjoying her new and exciting life that she had little time to worry or care about what I was doing.

Jim hardly ever spoke to me and certainly didn't want to hear my chatter, but I was so enamored of the "artistic life" that I didn't mind being ignored except when he wanted to get laid or use me as a model. His work was good and, of course, he painted me nude. His work is hanging in the Art Institute of Chicago, but I have never been able to ascertain whether any painting with me in it survived.

One Sunday we went to Sausalito to visit some of his friends from college who were living on a houseboat. There was a very pretty debutante/sorority girl that, I think, had known him in the old days and everyone there ignored me as a passing fancy, which of course I was. After several months even I got tired of being ignored and moved on. I don't think he noticed.

PETER

The next man on my road to discovery was gorgeous Peter who claimed to be the nephew of a famous writer. I met him through a modeling friend, and I said I wanted to meet someone ordinary and nice. Peter was nice but not ordinary. He taught English at a private boys school and was the perfect gentleman, just what I needed after the bohemian life. He kissed me when delivering me back to Nob Hill but never even made a pass, which was nice. Finally, a man who enjoyed my company with no apparent strings attached. He was tall, dark and handsome. He wore clothes beautifully and always looked so perfect that I wondered what he saw in me. After we had been going out for a week or so he asked me to go with him for a weekend to a cabin he owned in Healdsburg on the Russian River. It sounded like an adventure, walking in the woods, looking in the quaint shops in the village. The wooden cabin was beautiful with a small living room, large kitchen, and bedroom. He was meticulous and the place was spotless. It was decorated with antiques and old quilts and felt very rustic and homey. As soon as we arrived and started putting the groceries we had brought away, he asked me to put on a rubber apron that I had noticed hanging by the sink. I really thought it was weird but complied and darned if he didn't get an immediate hard-on. Groceries forgotten, he rushed me into the bedroom and made love while his three slobbering dogs sat at the foot of the bed watching us get it on. It was a little disconcerting and hard to achieve the mood with onlookers. Fortunately, it was over very fast and, apparently satisfied, he patted me on my flank like I was a good dog and went to finish storing the food. I lay there hardly spent and watched the dogs watch me. Finally, I got up and went to help Mr. Rubber Apron.

As he explained to me later over dinner, "I have a fetish and after many years on the couch discovered that the only time my mother ever showed me any affection was when she was cooking." She was from Germany and evidently many a household had these rubber aprons in their kitchens. He went on, "She wore that rubber apron every night and when I came home from school she would run over and give me a big hug and sometimes a kiss and always a piece of cake she was making or a cookie." I had never heard of such a thing at that time but was fascinated by his theory. He continued, "One night when I was about 14, I wandered into the kitchen to get a drink of water and saw the apron hanging there on its special rack. I thought of my mother and on a whim, pulled the apron off its rack, held it next to me and masturbated." I actually had heard enough but he went on, "When I was old enough to date, I discovered I was impotent. I would go home after the date completely undone but there was the apron waiting for me, to sooth me and make everything OK." He took a breath. I just wanted to go home. "Finally," he said, "I met a girl I really liked and confided in her. She suggested that I bring the apron and see if maybe she wore it something would happen. Yes!" He jumped up in excitement. "I was able to have a normal sex life from then on." I didn't think there was anything at all normal about it, but to each his own. I enjoyed his company otherwise and continued seeing him for a few months. During that time, I met a few of his ex- girlfriends and each of them had a rubber apron hanging in a prominent place in the kitchen. I guess they kept it as a reminder of why they were exes.

One evening I invited him to come to my parents' apartment to have dinner. I had mentioned to my mother that I was dating a teacher who was the nephew of a famous writer. She was always impressed by anyone who had anything to do with celebrity and was anxious to meet him. I didn't tell her about his fetish, although in retrospect that also might have intrigued her. He arrived on the appointed night and right away made an indelible impression on my mother by complimenting her taste in the décor of the beautiful apartment. He also brought her favorite candy and a large bouquet of flowers. Peter certainly knew his way around a woman. The two of them kept up a lively conversation with my father and I sitting back just watching mother work her magic. When dinnertime came, Peter, without a minute's hesitation, took my father's place at the head of the table. Politeness kept the peace, but it was a crass thing to do and my father, to his credit, didn't say anything. I finally saw that, weirdness aside, he was egocentric and not a person for the long haul.

UP UP AND AWAY
1954-1955

I was getting tired of modeling and decided that the perfect job for me would be the glamorous life of a stewardess. After work one day, I went to the United Airlines headquarters in San Francisco and made my application. Soon, I was called to come for an appointment. I showed up at the allotted time and was ushered into a nicely furnished office. Behind the desk was a very handsome man, dressed in a suit. He asked me a few questions then told me to walk across the room and pretend he was an unruly passenger whom I was to placate. Having had to placate many an unruly rag salesman I had no trouble at all in getting the pretend fellow to calm down. I was an actress after all. The man behind the desk seemed extremely pleased, asked me a few more questions and had me fill out another form. After he read it, he said, "Do you think you can be ready to go to Omaha next week for training?" Oh, my goodness. How exciting! I would meet movie stars or a prince and live the rest of my life in splendor.

He said there was only one little test I would have to pass...the EYE TEST! Well, I was blind as a bat. I knew that stews weren't allowed to wear glasses because of appearance and secondly, air safety. I was screwed. I made an appointment with United's eye doctor and prayed. When he finished the test, he looked at me and said, "Your vision is 20/200. You are legally blind!" Well, I knew that of course but in my most dramatic way I begged him to do something, that I had wanted to be a stewardess since I was a little girl, and my heart would break if I couldn't fly the friendly skies.

He took pity on me and said that if I could get an eye doctor in the city to say I had 20/30 eyesight, he would pass me. I jumped up, kissed him and took off to find a crooked eye doc. Finally, I heard of a guy who had lost his practice due to alcoholism and was giving eye tests to the bums down on the Tenderloin. I went into a really dingy office of sorts and explained what I needed and that I would pay him fifty bucks to lie for me. I told him I needed 30/20 eyesight.

Even in his addled state, he was confused, "Are you sure that's the number they gave you?"

"Quite sure," I muttered. He wrote out the prescription and I hopped a cab to the airport. When I got in to see the doc, he looked at the prescription, and sadly shook his head. I burst into tears but knew there was no way he could pass me. He offered me any ground job. I declined and left dejected and furious with myself for being so stupid.

SALLY
1954-1956

I had gotten involved in a small theatre in the North Beach area and was elated to finally be back to where I felt I belonged. It was fun to be in the heady atmosphere of a theatre again. It didn't matter to me that most of the actors had day jobs and were not professionals because I had a day job too and certainly wasn't a professional. But we all had one thing in common, a love for the theatre. I auditioned for and got the part of The Strega in Tennessee Williams's play *The Rose Tattoo*. It was a very small part, but I enjoyed just being included.

My job with Crystal was a good job and I enjoyed it, but it afforded little of the adventure that I craved. Little did I know that in only a few weeks I would meet a young woman who would change my life completely and catapult me into an entire new world of adventure. Her name was Sally Lacey and she told me that she had just returned from Hollywood where she had been featured in several Lash La Rue films. He was known as "The King of the Bullwhip." He made extremely low budget westerns for a rather shady film company. Sally said she eloped with him after a very boozy night. Lash had been married by his count at least ten times so it's very possible he married Sally. Evidently, as she told it, when they sobered up, she had second thoughts and the marriage was annulled.

Sally usually wore white, was flamboyant and moody. She was always concerned about money, but nevertheless spent whatever she had on clothes and the club life. We became fast friends and went out almost every night on the town. She was the beautiful girl I always attached myself to, vain and self-involved. She was even more adventurous than I and the degree of excitement we generated when we were together was heady. The City was really hopping then…Dave Brubeck at The Cellar, Johnny Mathis, when he was a nineteen-year-old track star at San Francisco State, at Ann's 440 singing "Hard Hearted Hanna." It was a heady time actually seeing Phyllis Diller in one of her first shows at the Purple Onion dissing her husband, "Fang."

Sally's mom, a very sweet and lovely woman, lived out near the cliffs, which was on the western edge of San Francisco, near the beach. The area was named after The Clift House, built in 1863 by Adolphe Sutro where the wealthy could come to the ocean and dine. For the poor population, he built The Sutro Baths, an amazing glass-roofed structure containing seven saltwater pools. They were still standing when I was there but had been abandoned.

Sally's mom had long since given up on Sally settling down, having a family and a husband who would be a good provider. Sally's father had been tragically killed in a boating accident. He had been a prominent judge in the area but evidently hadn't saved or maybe gambled all the money away as Sally and her mom were barely scraping by. My parents became friends with Ethel and would have her come into the

City for lunch or dinner. They liked Sally but thought our relationship might be "more than friends," so they insisted I go to a psychiatrist to find out if I was a lesbian. It was really weird, considering what happened seven years later. He kept probing, asking stupid questions.

"Do you know what homosexuality is?"

"Sure, I have a lot of gay friends."

"Do you think you may be in love with your friend."

"What!? No, I love her like you love a best friend, you know."

"Have you ever seen her naked?"

"No."

"But, you're in hotel rooms...what happens there?"

"We always go in the bathroom to get undressed. Sally's always going on about how ugly her breasts are...she'd be too embarrassed to let anyone see them."

"But you would like to see them?"

"Gosh, no."

"Have you ever had sexual thoughts about Sally?"

"Good God, NO! Jesus, this is ridiculous."

I got up and walked out the door. I don't know what the shrink told my parents, but the subject didn't come up again. Later, when I came out, I thought about Sally and me and yes, I was attracted to her verve, the glamour, the excitement she generated, the fun we had but never sexually.

Sally had a lover who was a big shot with Collier's encyclopedias. He was a very sharp character. Used to "shoot his cuffs." He was handsome in a sexy sort of way, heavy set with fine features, slightly balding and perfect white teeth. He taught Sally the business as well as giving it to her and she taught me. I quit my modeling job with Crystal and began my new career. First, we went door to door around the San Francisco area, and as we got better at our pitch, we decided to take it on the road. Sally drove a white Porsche convertible that she called her "White Plume" from *Cyrano*. It was a really snazzy car and we were pretty snazzy too. My parents, who had pretty much left me alone since we moved, were not happy about my new occupation. They thought modeling was a much better sounding occupation than encyclopedia salesgirl.

We had a terrific pitch. Knock, Knock… "Good morning/afternoon Ma'am" (we always tried to hit housewives…you could usually tell by all the toys on the front lawn). "My name is Patricia Crowder and I am in your area for a few days and would love to talk to you about an educational breakthrough for you and your family. Is your husband home?" If he were at work, we would make an appointment for that evening and come back as it was always the husband who had the money but the wife who had the desire.

We would show up at the appointed time in our jaunty hats and white kid gloves and proceed to cover the entire living room floor with fabulous glimpses of the knowledge that they and, of course, their children would acquire if… "For only ten dollars a year for ten years you can buy the yearbook which will keep your and your children's newly acquired knowledge up to date." It sounded too good to be true which, of course, it was as they actually had to lay out two hundred and fifty dollars up front to ensure the speedy delivery of their yearbooks. It was truly amazing to see family after family shell out their hard-earned money for something that might or might not be used. Being somewhat altruistic I hoped that I was really helping someone and that they were not just "mooches," as our esteemed leader called them.

We decided to go up north and the first stop was Portland, Oregon. I had my twenty-first birthday in Portland at a nightclub where there was funny lighting that made your teeth look really white or maybe it was the fact that Sally turned me on to my first marijuana cigarette.

We had picked up another salesman named Martin and he and I became an item. Martin had a monkey that traveled with him and that goddamned monkey hated me. At every opportunity, especially when Martin and I were making out, that damn monkey shit on me. Martin was about five feet tall with the ego of a giant, a real piece of work. I finally realized that I had put up with his and his monkey's shit for way too long and the three of us parted company.

About the same time, Sally broke up with the boss for the third or fourth time, and she and I took off to Utah where we hit the lumberjack camps. The axers would greet us with coffee cans filled with money, they were so desperate for reading material.

I never feared for my safety the whole time I was on the road, or even in the burbs of San Francisco. It was 1955 and most of the people we hit were working class people, just trying to make a better life for their kids. Even in the camps with the woodsmen, we never felt any anxiety or threat. We never dressed provocatively or acted in any manner that would suggest we were "asking for trouble." We gave the impression of nice, well-bred girls who were coming into their homes to bring their families' gifts of knowledge. The entire experience was heaven for a while, but after a few months I got tired of door-to-door and living in hotels and motels and we headed back to the City.

Sally suggested we go see a psychic she had heard was simply fabulous so off we went. The woman saw Sally first while I waited nervously in the small hall. When Sally came out, she rushed by me without saying anything. I really didn't want to go in because of Sally's reaction but curiosity got the better of me. I entered a parlor that was straight out of the Victorian age. The furniture and furnishings were very ornate. The mustiness of the air coupled with the faint odor of musk while, not unpleasant, was omnipresent. The woman was sitting at a round table covered with a colorful patterned shawl and asked me to sit across from her. She was dressed in a long gown that was decorated with faux jewels. She wore her long grey hair in a bun that had a jeweled comb jutting out of it. Her hands were wrinkled, and her fingers covered in rings. She really did look like a gypsy. She had a pack of Tarot cards that she shuffled and asked me to cut. She then laid some out and began to tell my fortune. She knew nothing about me, yet she seemed to know everything. She knew that I had wanted to be a stewardess and the whole story of why I wasn't accepted, and she said, "You should never fly. You could be killed in an airplane crash!" The whole experience was pretty amazing and especially the part about the airline. I wanted to share what the psychic told me with Sally, but she didn't want to talk about it so pretty soon the whole thing was forgotten.

Sally and I continued to go out, but she started going out with a guy who was into heavier drugs and slapping Sally around and as Sally's drug and alcohol use increased, we drifted apart.

FLASH FORWARD
1972

I heard from my parents that Sally was in really bad shape. Apparently, she had shown up at my father's office, dirty and crying. He gave her a few bucks out of pity but then I heard that she had borne a child and had moved back in with her mother. One night while Sally was out, her mother fell asleep holding a cigarette and both she and the child burned to death. I was shocked by this tragedy and just couldn't believe that my beautiful Sally could possibly fall so low and I was able to contact an old mutual friend who said she had heard Sally was living in Sausalito and not doing well.

I had to see for myself, so to the delight of my twelve-year-old daughter we got in our old car and took off for Sausalito. We spent the first night at The Madonna Inn in the Old Water Mill Room. My daughter was over the moon with the large replica of a water mill gushing out all night long until she finally fell asleep and I could turn the darn thing off. The next day we arrived in San Francisco, checked into our hotel and took a tour of what I remembered of the City. I showed her our apartment on Nob Hill, North Beach, Lombardy Street, Chinatown, and everything I thought she might be interested in. The next day we crossed the Golden Gate Bridge to Sausalito. I went to the police station, thinking they might have an address. When I told the officer on duty her name, he sighed,

"Ah, now lady, that's not a good idea." When I questioned him further, he reached into a drawer and pulled out a file. Sally had several arrests for drunk and disorderly, soliciting, public nuisance, etc., etc. In spite of his protests, he gave me the address warning me to be careful.

We drove to a run-down dilapidated house and after getting no answer at the door, I told my daughter to stay in the car with the doors locked and then I walked to the back of the house. I opened the door and walked into a nightmare. The place was filthy and there were several people, obviously drunk or stoned lying on the floor or on dirty mattresses. I asked the only one who seemed somewhat coherent where Sally was. He mumbled something about a party and being back soon. I decided that after all the trouble I had gone to find her, I would wait. I retrieved my daughter from the car and with misgivings took her into the disaster zone. Our coherent host offered us a swig out of his bottle and after politely declining we sat down on a nasty couch and waited. About an hour later the door opened and a creature that had once been the beautiful Sally reeled in, hair matted, dirty bare feet, teeth missing and wearing a once white long tattered dress. There was an askew tiara atop her head, and she was carrying an approximately four-year-old child who was obviously mentally retarded, probably due to alcoholic fetal syndrome. I said, "Hi Sally, it's Pat." She looked at me as though at a stranger as she put the child on the floor then as comprehension dawned, she covered her mouth with her hand and gasped, "Pat, oh my God." She looked away from me and started babbling about the party and having to feed the baby, whereupon she grabbed a can of beans from the bare pantry, opened it and gave it to the child who hungrily ate the beans with her dirty stunted fingers.

Sally sat down on the floor in front of us, grabbed my hand with her discolored, broken-nailed hands and began weeping. After she recovered somewhat, she said, holding her hands in front of her broken mouth, "You know, Pat," she said, "any day now I'm getting some money from a guy I know and I'm getting my teeth fixed." She said she was going to come to L.A. and get back in the business. I told her I would like to help her in any way that I could, but it broke my heart to see how my once beautiful, beloved Sally had destroyed herself and the life of another.

My daughter said, "Mom, can we go now?" She was clearly upset by what she had seen.

I pulled her close to me and whispered, "It's okay Puss, just a few minutes more."

Sally looked at me, and then my daughter and mumbled, "It's not a very good day. Maybe you could come back tomorrow. I've just gotta get myself straight. Could you lend me a few bucks?"

I said, "Sure Sally, whatever you need." I gave her ten dollars, pulled her up off the floor, hugged her, smoothed her hair and walked out of her sordid, hopeless life. I cried all the way back to Los Angeles.

THE ALLEY
1956-1957

I had grown used to doing what I wanted, when I wanted, which up to a point had been OK with my parents as I was of age, but it was not an ideal situation, so I decided that I would like to return to Houston to pursue acting in a serious way. My mother, in particular, thought this was a good idea. She had changed somewhat in our relationship. I wouldn't say love but there was an approval of my newfound self-confidence, and an awareness of the way I looked and put myself together. She could now show me off to her friends.

I called Nina Vance, the director of the Alley Theatre who had been encouraging when I had apprenticed. I asked her if I would be welcomed back and she said that would be up to me as there was always room for volunteers to clean the toilets and work the front of the house. I jumped at the chance. I got a job at Foley's Department store modeling at lunchtime for all the ladies who lunched and started working at the theatre in the evenings doing whatever was necessary. After several months of hard work, Nina made me an associate member of the staff, hanging lights and working in the booth.

I finally got a part in *Anniversary Waltz*, playing Janice, a small but cute role. I did my best to make my scene stand out and indeed one of the reviewers said that I "wiggled my way on and off the stage very well!" Dreams of Marilyn! The actors jobbed in for this production were Neil Hamilton, a pioneer performer in silent films and the "talkies," having appeared in the first two "Tarzan" films. He came with his wife, a demure woman whom he referred to as "Mommy." Strange relationship. The other actor who came from New York was Ethel Shutta who had been in The Ziegfeld's Follies and appeared opposite Eddie Cantor in *Whoopee*. I felt very privileged to actually be on the same stage with such a luminary. She later, at the age of seventy-four, originated the part of Hattie Walker in Sondheim's smash hit, *Follies*, in which she stood stock still in the middle of the stage and belted out "Broadway Baby." I have seen *Follies* a number of times but no one, in my opinion, was able to hit those lyrics like she did. I continued doing small parts and learned lighting design and operation from Jimmy Jeter, one of the stalwarts of the theatre.

Nina chose to mount *Julius Caesar* using New York actors instead of using the company. She brought down Philip Lawrence, the director of the Shakespearewrights, a fine Off-Broadway theatre, to direct. The actor playing Caesar became ill, so Phillip assumed the role as well as directing. He had a broad English accent, and it was quite a shock to discover that he was not from the "olde" country but originally from Searcy, Arkansas.

West Side Story had just opened on Broadway and Phillip would stand in the wings before curtain, amusing us all by a hysterical version of "I Feel Pretty" while showing off his toga. The Brutus jobbed in was a fine actor known mostly for the soap, *One Life to Live*. He had an amazing career working with the likes of Luther Adler, Paul Robeson, Jose Ferrer, Katherine Hepburn and Yul Brenner. He was drop-dead gorgeous and fluttered many a young apprentice's heart with hope, among them my best friend Penny who fell hard for him. I tried to warn her that this type of man loves and leaves but she was sure he was in love with her. The fact that he lived in New York and was probably married did not deter her. She was determined to go to New York to be with him. Evidently, he had casually said if she was ever in New York, to look him up sometime. I really felt sorry for her, as I knew the outcome of this fantasy would result in heartbreak but it's hard to reason with a young woman in love.

The actor who was hired to play Cassius, Theo, really did have that lean and hungry look with his handsome pock-marked face, tall with a noble bearing and a beautiful voice. He had been in the company of The Shakespearewrights playing Claudius in *Hamlet* and Malvolio in *Twelfth Night*. I was very attracted to him, or maybe it was Cassius, but we started dating and what was just a theatre affair soon became serious. He was a lovely man ten years older than I and had never been in a serious relationship before. I wasn't sure that I was really in love with him, but I was woefully insecure and in need of a strong man who I thought would take care of me. When the play was over, he asked me if I would come to New York to be with him.

So, without really thinking it through, I said yes. I would get an apartment with another girl or two, a job and we would continue our affair with possibly marriage as the end result. In my mind, my only thought was that not only could I be married, but I would finally be able to fulfil my desire to study acting in New York and become a working actress.

Alley Theatre director Nina Vance goes over a scene from "The Lark" with J. Frank Lucas and Pat Crowder.

Entre Nous **Backstage**

LONDON

1958

I had written to my parents about the New York Actor I had met and had fallen in love with and that I was going to move to New York. When they realized the seriousness of the affair and that he was a YANKEE/JEWISH/ACTOR, I was promptly invited to go with them to England where my father was to teach the glue-cleaning process he had invented to one of the major chemical companies there. The idea they came up with was to keep my mother company while my father was working but mostly to get my mind off of Theo. I actually didn't know which they thought was worse, the Jewishness, the acting or the Yankee part.

This brings up a strange pattern of behavior on their part. Often, to get me to do what they wanted, money or some expensive gift would be offered. I think they saw these offerings as gifts of love instead of bribes. Unfortunately, I was never taught about developing good character traits; loyalty, truthfulness, selflessness, accountability and self-control were certainly not part of my upbringing. When I first came back to The Alley, I lived close to the theatre in a nice inexpensive apartment I could afford on my modeling salary. Erroneously thinking it was an unsafe neighborhood, they showed up with a car, and the keys to an apartment on the other side of town for which they would pay the rent. Displaying my lack of character, I greedily accepted instead of holding my ground. And, of course, I'm sure they paid for the first-class tickets for my part of the trip to get me away from Theo. I again agreed mainly because I really wanted to go and dismissed any shame in accepting another bribe. I wrote to Theo that I was going with them and would come to New York after that.

I took a plane to San Francisco to meet my parents where we boarded the Pan Am Stratocruiser bound for London. We flew to Gander, Newfoundland where we crossed the icy tarmac and into the small terminal while the plane was being refueled. After refueling was completed we got back onto the plane where sleeping berths for the first-class passengers had been set up. We were able to change into our nightclothes in the much larger lavatories than are now on planes and climb into our nice warm curtained cubbies for a six- or seven-hour snooze.

When we arrived, we were whisked off to The Savoy where my father's hosts had installed us and while my father worked we saw the town, courtesy of the personal chauffeur provided by our hosts. We saw the newly installed Queen at The Trooping the Colour. She rode her beautiful stallion right by us, and I was duly impressed and amazed that she was actually quite lovely and that photos of her didn't do her justice. We toured Buckingham Palace and spent hours in the London Museum. Amazingly, Mother and I got along really well, and we actually had a good time and I felt thrilled to be, for a while, the recipient of her fun, wit and intelligence.

We went shopping. Mother, an inveterate shopper, was

always most approachable when looking through the racks. We could talk about this label or that or whether the garment was becoming or not. The closest we ever got to a real mother-daughter relationship was when rushing up the escalator together to buy sale items.

In London, the pound at that time was much lower than the dollar so we bought cashmere sweater sets and perfume at Harrods, the famous department store that had absolutely everything from clothes to dogs to an amazing food court. We went to the Ritz for tea, and I was introduced to the practice of putting the milk in before the tea and how to properly pour the liquid gold.

PARIS AND GERMANY

Mother wanted to visit Paris, a lifetime desire, and also to go to Heidelberg, Germany. We took the ferry across the English Channel and when we got to France, a train into the fabled city of Paris. It was certainty more beautiful than even I had imagined it, and we saw as much as we could in the few days we had there.

We went to the Eiffel Tower and we discovered that we were both afraid of heights. Just going up that strange elevator gave me the willies. We went to The Louvre and could have spent a week there but managed to see the Mona Lisa and many amazing paintings up close, not just reproductions in an art book. We walked around the Notre Dame Cathedral and thrilled at the sight of the enormous stained-glass windows. Mother bought tickets to the famous Folies Bergere where we watched in awe as semi-naked and naked entertainers danced and cavorted about the stage and swung over us on giant swings. We both felt like we were Scarlett on first seeing the delights of that beautiful city, grasping and greedy.

We then took a train to Frankfurt, Germany, changed trains and went to Baden-Baden to stay at the famous Brenners Park-Hotel and Spa. Mother, always fascinated by the Royals, had read that King Edward the VII had stayed there as well as the King of Siam in some long-ago history and wanted to experience the atmosphere and ambiance. The hotel had been closed during the war, was still undergoing reconstruction and certainly was not the grand palace she had imagined. We were shown to our room, little more than a closet with two twin beds. When we retired for the night after a lovely dinner we discovered, to our dismay, that the beds consisted of a thin mattress that was secured by a rope foundation. It was the most uncomfortable bed in which I had ever tried to sleep although the very cozy goose down comforter helped some. The next day, at lunch, I was just about to cut up the gorgeous, fresh white asparagus, when a stiff-coated waiter approached me, "Nein, nein fraulein, der Spargal" here he waved his fingers in the air, "der fefingern, der fefingern." Oh, OK. I gingerly picked up a large spear and put it in my mouth while der Ober watched with satisfaction.

We took a train to Heidelberg in the afternoon and while on the train mother began to feel ill. At times she suffered from an attack of the Crohn's disease that had almost taken her life almost ten years before. By the time we got to Heidelberg she was doubled up in pain. We went right to the hotel and she got into bed. I tried to sooth her, offering tea and sympathy, but she told me to just leave her alone and go sightseeing. I, of course, took my aborted ministering as rejection, but she probably just wanted to be alone. I took a tour to the fabulous castle and a ride on the Rhine and later bought a Nikon camera. When I got back to the hotel, she had called my father and arranged for us to return to England where a doctor recommended by the company would be waiting for her. Since we hadn't had time to unpack our bags, we rang for the porter who called a taxi and back we flew to London.

LONDON REDUX

Mother started feeling better once we got back to London, after having seen the doctor, and was ready to hit the town again. We saw *Duel of Angels*, a play by Giraudoux, starring Vivian Leigh and Mary Ure. Talk about seeing your fantasy come true! There, only two rows in front of me was SCAR-LETT! Oh my God. Never in my wildest dreams could I ever have imagined that I would actually see my fictitious heroine up close and in person. She was even more beautiful in person than in film. She didn't have a southern accent, but she was and would always be for me, Scarlett! After the theatre, on the way back to the hotel, Mother and I talked some about our mutual absorption with Scarlett. She said how much she loved the film and how faithfully it portrayed the South at that time. I avoided contradicting her as I didn't want to stop the conversation. She went on to talk about Scarlet and Ash-ley and Rhett and how she didn't like the ending. I asked her if she could relate to Scarlett as a survivor. She said, "What are you going on about?"

I said, "Well, you know how you survived your father's leaving and living in a tent."

She spat out, "Why are you always talking about the past? I don't ever want to hear anymore about the past!" By that time, we had arrived back at the hotel, and the conversation was over, done! I believe she related strongly to Scarlett's survival instinct, just as I did. I was thrilled to discover that we had something besides shopping in common, but it would never be examined as so many things weren't. I longed my whole life to have a meaningful conversation with her, but her emotions were locked so deep inside that it was impossible. I have a recording of their 70th Anniversary. They were both affable, laughing, having fun with their friends. At the end of the party, after everyone left, I continued taping. They sat on opposite ends of the sofa and when I tried asking them a few questions about how they met and fell in love, there were only glum faces and stony silence. The party was over!

One evening while in the hotel elevator, who should get on but Nina Vance. She promptly invited us out to Hammersmith with her to see a play starring the infamous Micheál Mac Liammóir who had founded The Gate Theatre in Dublin. The play was terrible, but in the pub afterward there was one amazing story after another. Mac Liammóir famously said, "I'm like Emily Bronte, without the genius of course …and… my own company as a general rule entrances me." Oh, the Irish!

One night my parents and I were invited by the president of the chemical company to go with him and his wife to their club. There were drinks in the drawing room of the lovely old establishment then dining and dancing. It was all very British and proper upper class. I chatted with Earl so-and-so on my left and Lady so-and-so on my right and tried to keep up my end of the conversation as best I could, given the fact that I could hardly understand a word said to me. People began to dance and a very handsome and elegant man wearing a bespoke suit and sporting a turban on his head approached me and asked me to dance. He was a Maharaja of somewhere and danced beautifully. He asked me questions about myself and unlike my usual outpouring of whatever might be on my scattered brain, I was too awed to actually respond with anything resembling intelligence. I was probably the most boring dance partner he had ever encountered but dance on we did until finally the band stopped playing and he led me back to my table, bowed and said, "It's been most interesting."

As soon as I sat down, Lady so-and-so leaned over and whispered, "How could you dance with that filthy 'ni—ger?'"

After closing my mouth that had been hanging open in shock, I managed a weak, "Well, he seemed very nice," whereupon Lady so-and-so turned away and never spoke to me again. I hadn't realized that so much hatred remained after India's independence. It disgusted me. I'll never know how I managed to escape the bigotry so prevalent in my own environment but somehow, I seemed to know from an early age that something was wrong with such attitudes.

All too soon it was time to leave. My parents, to lure me away from the hated boyfriend, said they would send me all expenses paid to the Royal Academy of Dramatic Arts assuming, of course, that I would even be able to get in. So, the one time I stood my ground and said no turned out to be a huge mistake, especially if I were really serious about becoming an actress. They were not happy campers but to save the day, Mother was informed that we would be returning to New York by ship and First Class, no less. We went shopping.

THE MAURITANIA

The *Mauritania II* was built in 1938, but shortly after her initial sailing, Hitler's armies invaded Poland, the Second World War started and the ship was requisitioned by the British government for use as a troop ship. In 1947 she was retrofitted back to a luxury liner.

The interior of the ship featured what was known then as "Late Art Deco Style" furnishings and furniture, which in 1947 would have been the height of luxury but by 1958 looked a little dowdy as Swedish Modern was all the rage. The First-Class grand hall was two stories tall with a beautiful glass dome at the top and in the middle of the hall stood the fabulous grand staircase that was just made for "sweeping down" which I did as often as I could, fox stole dragging behind.

Most of the staterooms in first class had a small bathroom with a shower, twin beds with a nightstand between and a small porthole (no verandas here). There was a small wardrobe that really wasn't big enough for all the formal clothes that were required every night. The people who traveled back and forth in this manner took large trunks that had hangers and drawers for all their paraphernalia and could be set up in their stateroom.

First Class could only be afforded by the wealthy, and I certainly did my best to liven up our table of tired businessmen who flirted outrageously with me while their bored, jaded women had another martini.

During the day, there were deck games such as shuffle-board, deck tennis and, of course, dancing. There was an indoor pool, but as I had not packed a swimsuit, I did not indulge.

Second class or Tourist was for upper middle-class people and was perfectly acceptable. There was a nice dining room, and there were parlours and activities on the deck.

Third Class was very basic in its décor and furnishings. The first time I ventured down I was thrilled to see so many people in my age group. Kids on their way back from whatever travels they had been on and people of all ages coming to America to start a new life. There was such joy there, music and dancing. It was so very different from the frozen atmosphere of "above deck." I reveled in the native dances and music and beer, lots of beer. I met a young man from Poland who didn't speak English and I no Polish, but music and dance and youth transcend any language barrier and we managed to communicate very well. His name was Peter. He was handsome and intense. His black eyes and dark hair that fell over his forehead were very enticing and tempting. We had a lot of fun but with fond farewells I toddled back to the safety of my first-class suite and fell into bed exhausted. The next day, Mother wanted to know where I had gone. When I told her, she was thrilled. She wanted to hear everything about this boy I had met. It was very clear she would have sold me on the open market just to keep me from marrying Theo.

She said, "Oh, that sounds nice. Why don't you go down there every night for the rest of the cruise and leave us old fogies up here?"

I said, "Mother, you know I'm in love with Theo. Why can't you just accept that? He's a wonderful man and I'm sure you and Dad will love him when you get to know him."

She brushed by me on her way out the door, "He's not for you," she said. "He's not one of us!"

I didn't think I was "one of us" either but it was clear that she was set against him and that no amount of argument or discussion would change her belief system. He was Jewish, we were not. What we were was never entirely clear. Every week I was taken to the Baptist Church and dropped off at Sunday School ostensibly to learn the moral lessons I was not taught at home. When church was over, I was picked up and taken back home.

Every night in first class one dressed. By dressed, I mean tuxes on men and cocktail or evening gowns on women. Mother and I wore our new duds with verve and danced away the nights with the good-looking stewards who were assigned to dance/entertain the un-chaperoned women.

After dinner and dancing we played games. There was a horse racing game in which the stewards moved large figures of wooden horse heads, each of whom had a name, across the floor according to the number on the dice for each horse. There was heavy betting and a great deal of shouting and egging on their particular horse. It was all jolly fun, the money was flowing, the good times were rolling, and little did they know that the end of the class system was lurking in the shadow of time.

The crossing took six fabulous days and when we landed

at New York's Cunard Pier, there was Theo holding a beautiful bouquet of flowers. I introduced him to mother who was gracious enough to take us to Mama Leonie's for dinner. That night when we got back to his small studio Theo proposed, and I immediately said yes. I took a plane back to Houston, packed all my clothes, sold my car and took off for the Big Apple and another adventure.

NEW YORK
1958

Penny, my pal from The Alley decided to come with me to the big city in hopes of furthering her affair with the gorgeous Brutus. Soon after we got there she called, only to have a woman answer. A wife! Who knew?! Penny was devastated. She had lost her virginity to this cad and really believed he was in love with her. Penny was one of the most gorgeous women I had ever seen before or since. She looked almost exactly like Greta Garbo. She had the same delicate features set off by long rich brown hair. She was not graceful and was awkward regarding her appearance. She never wore makeup, and she tried to disguise her beauty by wearing hats and high-collared blouses and sweaters to cover as much of herself as she could. It was like covering the Mona Lisa, and though she was my best friend, it was hard not to be envious of such natural beauty.

Through a friend we got an apartment at 23 West 88th Street, right off of Central Park West. It was a very nice small one bedroom fifth floor walkup with a huge terrace. Now it would be considered a fabulous location, but then it was in the middle of Puerto Rican gangland. It was safer to go over to Central Park West and down to 86th Street, a very busy thoroughfare and then walk over to Columbus or Broadway.

I got a job at The Institute of Life Insurance as a librarian.

It was hard to get a full-time job if you were an aspiring actress, but fortunately the man who hired me had a sister who was an actress, and he understood the situation. It was a wonderful place to work. I had a desk next to a large window overlooking Madison Avenue and was surrounded by books. There was a real librarian, another girl, and our major tasks included taking phone calls from people who wanted information that was not readily available to them. Also, as part of my duties, I learned how to use a switchboard. It wasn't easy at first, and I frequently plugged in the wrong person or cut someone off. Some of the girls liked to listen in on certain conversations, but eavesdropping was strictly forbidden. Learning the switchboard and, of course, typing were two of the more useful and marketable skills I acquired and certainly came in handy in the years to come.

At around ten every morning, a boy would come around with coffee and pastries, and we would take a break to chat and gossip. It really was the perfect job. It paid just enough that I could afford my half of the eighty-dollar-a-month rent and food and still have a little left over for a new pair of shoes now and then. Best and Company was just around the corner from the office so after a quick lunch I would mosey over to check out the latest in what the debutants were wearing that season. I can still smell the coffee at Schrafft's, just downstairs in my building and see the beautiful red paper covered chocolate boxes with the blue and pink flowers painted on top.

The automat on 57th Street was my go-to place when a quick fix was needed. Put your dime in the slot of one of the built-in compartments and get a piece of pie and a nickel cup of coffee from another cubicle. There were small tables that were made for one or two, no lingering here. In and out was the idea. Sometimes on a nice evening, I'd buy a hot pretzel at the stand on the corner and while munching on the tangy softness stroll through Central Park in its lushness and smell the newly mowed grass. I loved being in the park, the city melting away. There were no worries then about being mugged or worse, and it was certainly better than the smelly subway unless it was cold when I exited at 86th Street and walked the two blustery blocks to our apartment.

Theo and I were having a wonderful time discovering each other and the city. He showed me the New York he knew, and I was in love with him and the city. We rode the ferry for a nickel, took the subway to Coney Island, went to the top of the Empire State building and walked, walked, walked. Heaven! Somehow, Theo got us really good seats for *West Side Story*! I knew all the words and music by heart and sat on the edge of my seat for the entire show. What a cast! What music! Oh Mr. Sondheim, the lyrics, and the dancing. Absolutely thrilling from the minute the overture started until that last mournful note. We walked out humming and dancing. We were Juliet and Romeo that night and, as it turned out, star crossed as well.

We set a date for a January wedding. Since Theo was Jewish and I wasn't we decided to have the wedding at The Ethical Culture Society.

Christmas was just around the corner and I was excited to see the beautifully decorated windows at Macy's and Tiffany's and the tree at Rockefeller Center. I had called my parents to tell them the date and they responded that they wouldn't be coming nor would they be responsible as parents of the bride to pay for any part of such an undertaking. I couldn't believe it. Their only daughter getting married and they were refusing to pay for the wedding or walk me down the aisle? They said if I were determined to marry THAT man, I could do it where they could invite their friends. "But Mom, my friends all live in New York."

"It's not about your friends," she said and hung up.

THE TRIP
1958

Penny wanted to go to Houston for Christmas, but she couldn't afford the train, so I said I would go with her on the bus, a two-day trip, hoping I could convince my parents to come to the wedding.

As we boarded on a very frosty New York morning, we made quite a pair. Penny with her army boots, thrift store parka and fatigues and I in my little high heel booties, a cute coat with a faux fur collar and a beret. It was tres chic for Greyhound. We settled in, chatting and looking out the window as we drove through the gritty streets of Manhattan and then onto the expressway and new adventures in bus land.

After a few boring hours in which we tried to nap and amuse ourselves with books we had brought, we arrived at the Washington, D.C. Greyhound bus depot. We got out to stretch our legs, go to the restroom and get some much-needed coffee. When we returned, we noticed that some new passengers had boarded. Among them was an old African-American woman holding a small child who was possibly three or four years old. They took the empty seats across from us, and I helped them put their things on the rack above them and we exchanged pleasantries. As we continued on our way, we learned that the child's parents had been killed in an automobile accident and that the woman was the child's grandmother who now had the task of raising her. Penny and I volunteered to help take care of Tina as the grandmother looked distraught and very tired. The grandmother readily agreed and promptly fell asleep as soon as I took Tina on my lap. She was an adorable child with neatly braided hair, bright alert eyes and a very large vocabulary for one so young. She quietly played with her doll on either my or Penny's lap and then fell asleep sprawled out between us.

We continued talking and admiring the scenery as we began our descent into the South. After several hours we took a rest stop in a small town in Virginia. There were no toilets on the buses in those days so every few hours the bus would stop at a gas station or small store so the passengers could relieve themselves and get a Coke or a candy bar. At breakfast, lunch and dinner we were given a half-hour to eat. The local bus stations usually had counters where you could have an egg or a sandwich. It was strictly fast food but still pretty good. We got off and started toward the restroom, Tina in my arms, when suddenly her grandmother rushed up beside us and took the child from me.

"You can't take her in there," she said pointing to the bathroom. I was about to protest when I saw the large sign WHITE ONLY and next to it pointing in a different direction COLORED. I was stunned. I had lived in the South most of my life, but the truth of the Black experience had never really touched me in my little sterile white world. When I lived in San Francisco, the few black people I knew were businessmen and women, artists, actors or musicians. I didn't see the separation that existed everywhere in our country. Separate and unequal. It was 1958 and still two years from the "Greensboro Four" sit-ins that changed the WHITE ONLY lunch counters at Woolworth stores to become the first department stores in the Southern United States to desegregate. I had a lot to learn.

When we got back on the bus, a very stout man gave me a dirty look as he sat down and took the vacant seat in front of me. I didn't think too much about it until he pushed his seat abruptly back hitting Tina in the head. I was about to berate the man when Tina spoke up, "That man didn't say excuse me and he got no hair neither!" Everyone within hearing distance broke up laughing at the man who promptly got up and moved to another seat. By this time, it was getting late and we were tired. I got up and took the seat that the man had vacated and lay Tina down on my seat. We all did the best we could to get a few hours of shut-eye.

The next morning, as we drove deep into the South and the beauty of The Carolinas, there were no more incidents and we settled into a routine of sorts. Penny said, "I think I'd like to come back here someday. Everything looks so peaceful."

Yes, it was serene and picturesque looking out the window at the fine old houses and the rows of cotton growing in the fields. At the rest stops and stations Tina's granny took her to the restroom and we would get food for all of us, either eating it on a bench outside the stop or on the bus. The afternoon of the second day we pulled into the Athens, Georgia Greyhound station. Penny scoped out the place and suggested taking Tina in with us to have a proper meal as it was a larger station and had a nice counter. The grandmother was definitely against this idea, but we honestly didn't see how anyone could possibly object to a little girl having a meal. We went into the station, Tina walking and skipping between us. When we got to the lunchroom we were stopped right away.

"You can't bring that 'ni—ger' in here," snapped the razor-thin, frizzy-haired blonde behind the counter. Several other people looked at us as though we were from Mars. We went back into the waiting room and decided that we would take turns eating while the other sat with Tina. Penny went first and although I wasn't seated in the "Colored" section, no one bothered us. Tina played with her doll and I kept vigil. Soon Penny came back with a grilled cheese and a shake for Tina and a burger for the grandmother who had opted to stay on the bus.

When Penny came back from giving Tina's grandmother her lunch, I went in to eat. Halfway through my repast I heard some sort of ruckus going on. A man in overalls and a straw hat yelling that "there was a real ugly gal in the waitin' room who had brought her 'pickaninny' into the station and was causin' a shit load a trouble for her and her 'n–ger" kid'."

I immediately got up and ran out of the lunchroom without even paying. Penny was standing in the middle of a gathering crowd holding Tina.

"What's going on Penny? What happened?"

"Some cracker in overalls asked me whose little 'n—ger' and I just said, she's mine!"

About that time overalls came running back towards us shouting, "Didja hear what she jest said?" Thet's her little 'n—ger'!" He started jumping up and down in front of us. "Thet's her little 'n—ger'….thet's her little 'n—ger'!"

The crowd grew closer and then they all began jumping up and down in unison, chanting "Thet's her little 'n—ger'…thet's her little 'n—ger'…."

Suddenly the bus driver pushed his way through the mob, yelling above the fray, "Get the hell out of here and get on the goddamned bus!"

We ran stumbling through the mob and onto the bus and the safety of our seats. The bus driver slammed the door, started the bus and as we drove out of the station we saw and heard rocks being thrown at us. Everyone on the bus was eyeing us suspiciously. Tina was crying and obviously terrified, as was I. Her grandmother came from the back of the bus where she had been asked to sit since we got into the South and gently lifted Tina up into her arms and carried her back with her. She never said a word, but we knew we would no longer be needed to help with the child.

"Why did you say what you did?" I whispered to Penny when the other passengers finally stopped staring at us.

"I just thought he was some dumb redneck asshole, not a maniac! It never dawned on me that it would cause a riot." Tears rolled down her beautiful face. "They could have hurt Tina," she sobbed. I turned away from her and her big mouth and looked out the window. I was sorry I had come on this nightmare of a trip with her. I could have been home already. Hurt Tina indeed, I thought to myself. If we hadn't gotten out of there when we did, we would probably be hanging from a tree by now, what an idiot! I ignored Penny for the rest of the day, and I just couldn't stop thinking of the consequences of our actions when we don't stop to think. But then, I had certainly said and done things that caused harm to others, so I really was in no position to judge. By dinner I was talking to Penny again though she remained quiet for the rest of the evening.

The morning of the last day of our trip we pulled into a large Greyhound depot in New Orleans. When we got off the bus to have breakfast, two men in suits approached us. They informed us that they were from the FBI and asked to see our passports. PASSPORTS! Penny and I looked at each other. She was as dumbfounded as I. We tried to explain that we were indeed American citizens and had actually been born in Houston, Texas.

"Wail," one of the men said. "What you done would indicate otherwise."

I blurted out, "Done, what done. I mean what did we do?"

"What you done," the other man said, "Was thet you two 'n—ger' lovin' gals jest bout caused a riot back there a ways and no patriotic American born young gals woulda acted lak thet!"

The first one spoke up, "We was thinkin' maybe you was commies!" I decided that it would probably be wise to go along with his skewed reasoning before we were deported to some Godforsaken place or maybe even Russia.

I punched Penny in the ribs as a warning to shut up and said, "Oh my goodness, Sir," I babbled. "As the good Lord is my witness, we never intended any harm. We were just trying to do the Christian thing by helping a poor old downtrodden Negro woman and her grandchild. It was a terrible mistake and if you kind gentlemen would just allow me to call my father, I'm sure he could satisfy your concern."

They looked at each other and the one who had been doing most of the talking said, "Wail, I recon thet won't be necessary. It seems like you thought you was doing a good deed so, for now, we're gonna let you go on your way.

"But," he added, "Ifen I was you two I'da think twice fore heping anymore 'n—gers', downtrodden or not!"

"Yes sir, thank you sir. We really appreciate your concern and promise to never again do anything so foolish."

Penny stammered out a thank you and we hurried back to the bus to more humiliation from the other passengers, muttering among themselves how we shoulda gone to jail, etc., etc. We looked back at Tina and her grandmother who averted her eyes. We sat down, looked at each other and burst into laughter, more like hysteria.

Penny said, "As the good Lord is my witness?"

"Look," I said, "You're the cause of all this so if I were you, I'd just say thank you and the good Lord too!"

"Yeah, you're right. Do you really think they were from the FBI?"

"No, I whispered. I think they were from the KKK!"

We finally got to Houston in the afternoon and were picked up by Penny's mom who asked us how the trip was. "Oh, just great," I said, looking at Penny. "Actually, pretty boring."

THE WEDDING AND AFTERMATH
1969

Nothing I could say would convince my parents that they should participate in any way in my upcoming wedding unless we married in Houston. They used the excuse that they couldn't afford it, but I knew that to be a lie. I was heartbroken. I begged and cajoled and did everything I could think of all to no avail.

I said, "Mom, none of our friends will be able to attend. They'd have to get there and then get a hotel."

She replied, "If your friends had real jobs instead of being bums it wouldn't be a problem for them to come to your wedding." She went on, "I told you it was just as easy to fall in love with a rich man as a poor one. You've made your bed, now lie in it!" Harsh words from a harsh woman. I was devastated but determined to make the best of it.

I went back to New York and began planning for the big day. I bought a very pretty short white dress on sale at Lord & Taylor and some white satin shoes. Penny helped me fix my hair and I gave myself a manicure. A package arrived from my mother. It was a beautiful but totally useless silk Peignoir set. It probably cost several hundred dollars that we certainly could have used. I could just see myself waltzing around our tiny apartment decked out in such regalia.

The wedding was on a very cold Saturday morning,

January 10th, 1959. The wedding was perfect. Theo's friends had chipped in to buy me a beautiful bouquet to carry, and after the wedding we went to Pam and Paul's apartment for our reception. Pam and the others at the reception had been classmates of Theo's at Carnegie Tech where he had gone to school after the war. His friends were mostly struggling actors and were wonderful and loving people. He was very lucky to have them in his life and then mine. They had all brought gifts for us and had made a potluck luncheon that was delicious. I had a wonderful time and certainly didn't let my parents' absence put a pall on the celebration. My new husband didn't say much about neither his parents nor any of his relatives coming to the wedding, but it must have been as painful for him as it was for me. It took a long time for them to accept me, as I was the only non-Jewish person to marry into their family, a Shiksa!

After the party, Theo had a big surprise for me. Somehow, he had saved eighty dollars and had booked a room at the Plaza Hotel. I was indeed surprised and thrilled. We arrived in a taxi, me in my wedding dress carrying a small bag and Theo in his brand-new navy-blue suit from Filene's. We walked up to the reception desk only to be told that our room was not available. Theo was so livid that he grabbed the poor clerk by the tie, pulled him across the top of the counter and began berating him at his impressive full volume as the poor man struggled to speak. He finally got out that we were to be upgraded to a suite and that we would be ushered to it immediately. Theo let go, straightened himself to his full height and said, "Yes, that's more like it."

We were shown into the most amazing suite I had ever seen. There were two bedrooms, separated by a large living room. A kitchen stocked with various goodies and an enormous bathroom that was larger than our entire apartment. I took a long and luxurious bath, put on my new Peignoir and went into the living room where a lovely supper had been set up, courtesy of The Plaza. After dinner we went into the gorgeous, huge bedroom for our sexy wedding night rites.

Unfortunately, Theo had turned on the TV where David Susskind was holding forth with his remarkable show, *Open End*. His guests that evening were Norman Mailer and Truman Capote. It was a very famous segment where Capote said of Mailer, "You're just a typist!" The show was indeed open ended and by the time it wrapped we were both too sleepy to "do it" and when we finally woke up the next day it was checkout time so our consummation at The Plaza was not to occur.

Theo had a studio apartment on 45th Street between 9th and 10th Avenues in Hell's Kitchen. To get to his apartment you had to walk through a long tunnel on the side of the main building that faced 45th and into an open courtyard and then into a back building and up several flights of stairs. The apartment was really a studio with a kitchenette and small second room used for storage. There was a separate toilet that had been built into the airshaft. When you had to go to the toilet in the winter, we kept an ice pick by the toilet to break the ice before you could go. He had a trundle bed which pulled out and a real fireplace that really came in handy on those freezing Manhattan nights with very little or no heat coming out of the radiator.

My handy husband had invented a shower contraption that consisted of an aluminum washtub to which he had welded a long aluminum pole and then had curved the top of the pole in order to hold a shower curtain. Ingenious! To take a shower you set the tub in front of the kitchen sink, attached a long rubber hose to the faucet, got into the tub, pulled the shower curtain around, reached out for the hose and turned on the water and got as wet as you could without filling the tub. Then, you turned off the faucet, soaped yourself and went through the whole thing again as quickly as possible. If too much water accumulated in the tub, it was impossible to pick up to empty into the sink, so a shower was certainly more of a necessity than a pleasure. Sometimes when I just couldn't face going through the whole rigmarole, I would just wash as best I could in the sink. Washing my hair was really a challenge but hey, the rent was $45.00 a month.

We soon discovered that two of us in such a small space was not congenial, to say the least, so I went out to look for a bigger place. We had decided that since I was working, we could afford as much as $80.00 a month. I found a place around the corner in a very nice apartment building (with a basement laundry!) on 44th Street between 9th and 10th Avenues right next door to The Actor's Studio. The apartment was on the first floor and faced the street on one side and a courtyard on the other. It was a very nice one bedroom with a real bathroom. I think I took an hour-long bath the day we moved in. It had a small living room and a large kitchen with room for a small table. Now I had to learn to cook! My mother had never allowed me in the kitchen so I literally couldn't even boil water. Theo could cook a few things but thought that the wife was supposed to be the cook. What he didn't seem to realize was that I was working all day, trying to shop for groceries on the way home and then supposed to get a full meal on the table at his appointed time. He had a lot more time on his hands than I did, but it was 1959 and that was the way it was in most working-class families and certainly he had been brought up that way. Another big issue was cleaning. I was supposed to check his clothing every day to see if they needed cleaning or laundry. I balked at this and we made a deal whereby he would put his soiled clothing on the bed, and I would take them to the cleaners or laundry and then pick them up when they were ready. The clothes that had to be washed I could put off until the weekend. Help was never offered, and I got the feeling that he felt that it was "beneath him." Theo explained the cleaning situation by telling me a story about his Grandfather, Jake and his Grandmother, Lena. If a wife wanted something done there was a method whereby she never directly asked for what she wanted but rather the husband had to think it was his own idea. If Lena wanted the drapes cleaned, she would come into the room where Jake was reading *The Daily Forward*, shake the drapes, say "Oy, the dust," and leave the room. A week or so would go by and she would enter the room, shake the drapes, "Oy, Jake the drapes are so dusty!" The next week when she came in and shook the drapes, Jake would look at her and say, "Lena, get these drapes cleaned. They're dirty." I was not brought up that way and really couldn't understand why there had to be so much deception. In my family if my mother wanted something as mundane as getting the drapes cleaned, she just called someone to come and clean them and my father never even entered into the equation.

I did find a wonderful meat shop in the neighborhood, Piccinini's on 9th Avenue who supplied the luxury liners and fine hotels with their meat. The owner was a lovely man named Rudy who always wore a hat with a feather stuck in the brim. I soon became friends with the women who shopped there, and they gave me tips on different dishes and Rudy himself would save a nice small piece of roast or lamb for a dollar or two and tell me exactly how to cook it.

Theo wanted me to meet some of his many relatives spread out in the New York region. The first relative I met was Theo's first cousin and best friend, Howard, at that time a New York Times correspondent. He was unhappily married with two small sons. They lived in New Rochelle and we visited them often. I learned to love herring and matzo balls. Howard and Theo would have loud and boisterous arguments, a family trait, both screaming at the top of their lungs with neither ever resolving anything.

Theo thought I should meet more of the clan who were also anxious to see the "Shiksa." We were invited to Connecticut to meet most of his very extended family. I was a nervous wreck and definitely wanted to make a good impression for his sake as well as my own. We sat down to dinner in a beautiful dining room, the table laden with all sorts of strange and interesting looking food. I had learned a few words of Yiddish, hoping to fit in and maybe drop an "Oy vey" into the conversation every now and then. There was an amazing dish that one of the aunts had made and I, using my new vocabulary, praised it as being "Khazeray" which I thought meant wonderful, but actually translates as "pig slop". Well, you could have cut the silence with a spoon. Then, thank heavens, everyone started laughing realizing I was just an idiot and not purposely offensive.

THE PLANE

Soon it was summer, and Theo got a job playing Cyrano at Bowling Green University in Ohio. The plan was that he would go, and I would join him during the run. It was near Detroit, so I would meet his parents who also had not attended the wedding as they truly had little money for travel. We had decided that we would go on to San Francisco to see my parents and then to Hollywood to check out the film scene as he had gotten a wonderful part on *The Naked City* playing the lead heavy and several agents from California had contacted him regarding representation. Since we were to be gone for a few weeks, I took a leave of absence from my job and got ready for a new adventure.

I got on a plane out of La Guardia and everything was going swell until we started hitting some pretty heavy turbulence. The pilot came on and announced that we were headed straight into a tornado, which he couldn't get around and to just hang on! God! It was horrible. We were flying upside down and the only way I knew that, since I couldn't see the horizon was that my seat belt became very tight and the stewardess was flat on the ceiling, or in this case floor. There were whiskey bottles whizzing through the air, purses airborne, and change floating in the air! Suddenly it stopped. The pilot came on again, "Well, folks, looks like we're flying in the eye right now but, sorry to say, we're going to have to go out of it and try to get to the other side of this thing. May God be with you!" Silence, no one screamed, no one tried to get out of their seats. Calm!

Out of the small airplane window, it looked like a scene out of *The Wizard of Oz*. There were flying objects, parts of what looked like rooftops and just then I thought of the fortuneteller's words, "You should never fly. You could be killed in an airplane crash!" Well, I thought, I guess this is it. Just then Hell began again. I grabbed the hand of the woman sitting next to me, but she had nothing to give me, no help and no human kindness. Just as she was peeling my death grip from her hand, the plane began to descend, and the turbulence smoothed out some.

"Well, folks," the pilot said, "Looks like we dodged a bullet that time. I'll have you on the ground in Detroit in about twenty minutes." Dead silence, then wild laughter, shouting, hugs. Even my unfeeling seatmate gave me a little smile. When we landed and walked down the steps onto the tarmac every single person knelt down and kissed the ground. The luggage was piled up helter-skelter and was a mess, but I finally found my bag. It was torn and open on one end, parts of clothing hanging out. But, thank God it was in good enough shape that I could pick it up and manage with both hands to get it to the terminal where my husband met me. Since the plane had been delayed, he had been worried, and no news had been forthcoming. I sat down, still shaking, and poured out the horrible story. All around us people were holding onto their loved ones and crying grateful tears.

DETROIT

Finally, I was calm enough to be led to a taxi and taken to Theo's mother and father's house in a suburb of Detroit. After a cursory hello, nice to meet you, I went into the guest bedroom, got into the bed fully clothed and slept until the next morning. When I finally got up there was no one home. Theo's parents had gone to work, and Theo had gone to the theatre according to a note he had left next to a box of cereal and some milk.

In the afternoon Theo came back, eager to show me the city. In those days Detroit was a beautiful and tranquil place. Nice homes, no graffiti on the buildings and a bustling downtown. His mom worked in a lady's dress shop and he dropped me off there while he ran an errand. It was a very nice shop with some lovely things, mostly for older women, not my style. She worked on commission and had to be competitive with the other two saleswomen. The rules were very strict. They weren't allowed to sit down, only had thirty minutes for lunch and no paid time off. She told me that her husband, Eli was a debt collector and went door to door in the greater Detroit area collecting money from mostly poor people who had gotten behind in their debts. Evidently, she told me, he had had a few close calls when certain people, whom I took to mean the blacks (Shvartses), had threatened him. Fortunately, nothing had ever happened, but she worried all the time about him. Theo came to pick me up and we went back to the house. He told me all about the play and how good the college kids were who were performing with him.

That night after his mom came home on the bus, she started dinner right away without changing or even washing her face. Soon, my new father-in-law came in without so much as a hug or kiss for his wife. Theo had told me that when he was growing up, he had never seen them show any affection to one another or to him, which partly explained why, in our own marriage, there was so little display of affection outside of the bedroom. My father-in-law sat down, got the paper and started reading it. I went in to help Theo's mom and when dinner was ready, we sat down with my father-in-law holding forth about his day and some of the amusing things that had happened. My new mother-in-law never said a word. After dinner she got up and immediately started cleaning up with no help offered from either man. I dried the dishes while she and I made idle chit-chat. When we were all finished, we went into the living room and she, for the first time since she had come home, sat down emitting a long sigh. Just as she began to get comfortable, her husband spoke up, "Get me an apple, Betty." No please, no thank you, nothing. She got up and brought him an apple and sat back down again. There was no conversation.

The next evening, we all went to Bowling Green to see *Cyrano*, which was a huge success. Theo was wonderful and the young cast delightful. Evidently his father had never seen him perform, as he had been less than enthusiastic about his son's chosen profession. About all he could manage when the play was over was a nod and a pat on the back but just that small amount of acknowledgement meant the world to Theo.

My husband had bought tickets for the plane to San Francisco but I had flatly refused to go. There was absolutely no way I was ever going to get on another airplane as long as I lived. Somehow, he got a prescription for Valium and, well-plied with tranquilizer, we took off for San Francisco with no turbulence, landed without incident and were met by my parents. They were gracious, thank God, and took us around and out to dinner several times. All in all, it was a good visit, although the YANKEE/ACTOR/JEW lurked in the background and we were both glad when it was over and we were on our way, with the help of my magic pills, to "Hollywood!"

HOLLYWOOD
1959-1962

Theo had arranged for us to stay at a famous "Actors Hotel," The Montecito, located right in the middle of Hollywood. There were studio apartments and one- and two-bedroom apartments available by the week or month. We rented a studio apartment for a week that took up quite a bit of our savings. The Montecito, a beautiful Art Deco building, had been built in 1931 and had been home to many famous and up and coming stars through the years, such as James Cagney, Mickey Rooney, Montgomery Clift and Ronald Reagan to name a few. I loved it there and enjoyed walking down the hill to Hollywood Boulevard to see all the famous landmarks. Grauman's Chinese Theatre with the footprints and signatures of all the famous movie stars that I had grown up watching. Musso and Frank's restaurant that had been a Hollywood tradition since 1919 where all the brilliant writers of the time had martinied and dined. The glamorous Roosevelt Hotel, the Brown Derby on Vine and Music City where you could listen to records in small glassed-in cubicles were all part of my daily meanderings.

Our neighborhood was fun, very safe and walk-able. While I was checking out the scenery, Theo was calling the agents who had seemed interested and signed with one who felt he could get him work right away.

After the week was up, we had to find another place as our funds were running pretty low. One of the other actors at The Montecito told us there was another actors apartment hotel on Vine called The Villa Elaine Apartment Hotel. We went to check it out. It was further down on Vine than I had walked, closer to Melrose and right across the street from an all-night market, The Hollywood Ranch Market. The market was, at that time, the only all-night market in Los Angeles or at least Hollywood and had a giant clock on top of the building whose hands moved around the face continuously. The huge sign above the market said, "We Never Close." There was also a twenty-four-hour doughnut stand on the corner of the market so you could have a doughnut whenever the need struck. When I got pregnant the smell of the rancid oil made me deathly ill and to this day, I really can't stand to even look at a doughnut.

The Elaine was a two-story building with a very nice entrance. There were some lovely duplex apartments with high ceilings in their large living rooms with a grand staircase to the second-floor bedroom. I was smitten but the rent was way out of our budget, so we had to opt for the studio apartment. What a letdown! It had a living/bedroom with a small, lumpy murphy bed, tiny bathroom and a kitchenette. The floor was covered with a disgusting green shag rug that had several suspicious-looking stains. It was awful but with little other choice we put down a week's rent and moved in.

The building was filled with mostly actors on the slow road to perdition. Many of the inhabitants had been semi-Broadway names, bit players in films of long ago and burlesque performers. In many of their rooms stood an open trunk just in case the all-important call came. It was sad and pathetic but somehow brave that the hope had never died.

We couldn't afford a TV, so we amused ourselves by turning out the lights to spy on the other denizens in the adjoining apartments. They were so close that we could actually hear and see everything that was happening and there was a lot going on...real drama. Oh Boy! There was a couple near the end that were both terrible drunks. She was a peroxide blond, strong as an ox and very tall. He was bald and at least a foot shorter than she. Every night they had a screaming match that usually ended with her picking him up and throwing him out of their second-floor window. He always landed in the bushes, got up and ran back upstairs yelling, "I'll get you this time, you son of a bitch!" Much better than TV! Right across from us was a beautiful young girl with long red hair and her mother. They had come to Hollywood for the girl to be discovered. As far as I could tell the only discovery that was made was a good-looking stud with a motorcycle who whisked her off every night leaving the mother to cry over a fruitless trip to La La Land. On the bottom floor there was a lesbian couple that regularly had knock down fistfights, lots of blood, then kiss and make up till the next time.

The swimming pool had been condemned but we all sat on beach chairs that had been placed around the now swampy hole where we traded stories. Ours was definitely the least interesting. There were scandalous stories of once-famous names on the burlesque circuit and what actress did what to another on a live radio show. We had our own, soon to become a name, Jackie Gayle keeping spirits up by his constant jokes and antics. I was enthralled by all the gossip and sad tales, but Theo refused to join us muttering something about sordidness. Maybe it was, but I sure as Hell was fascinated.

When Theo wasn't going out to the studios with his new agent, we explored with a car that the agent had loaned us until we could afford to buy one. Downtown LA at that time was the center of the universe. Everything was there. There were no malls in 1959 to speak of so everyone did all their furniture, clothing and household shopping downtown. There was a wonderful cafeteria called Clifton's that had a tropical theme complete with waterfalls. It fell into disrepair later but has now been rehabilitated to great acclaim. There were still trolleys running down the streets and in fact you could go all the way to the beach down Santa Monica Boulevard on a trolley, long since gone due to the influence of the car and tire industry.

Fancy stores lined Wilshire Boulevard. I. Magnin and Bullocks were where the movie stars shopped. Bullocks was in a magnificent Art Deco building with lovely furnishings from that time. When my mother visited, we went there to have lunch amid all the wealthy ladies who lunched and watched the fashion shows. Perino's Restaurant was down the street as was the famous Ambassador Hotel where the Academy Awards were first held in 1939 and Bobby Kennedy was shot in 1968.

One night, we walked down to Hollywood Boulevard to watch the comings and goings of the movie stars as they attended a premier at The Pantages, which was at that time strictly a film house. I forget the name of the film, but I'll never forget the excitement of the fans as all their favorite stars pulled up in their limos. One limo pulled up and a beautiful couple, all decked out in furs and diamonds got out. One of the fans pushed by me shouting, "Who is it... Who is it?"

Another fan yelled, "Oh, it's nobody!" Well that's Hollywood for ya.

I wanted to go back to New York as I thought Theo would have done very well in the theatre and the burgeoning television and film production there, and I could follow my dream of studying with Herbert Bergdorf and Uta Hagan. But Theo was not ready to give up his dream of La La Land riches and fame. When I finally accepted the fact that we were not returning to New York, I wrote to Penny asking her to send our things from our apartment in the city. Our apartment there was on the first floor and, evidently, I had left a window slightly open. When Penny opened the front door, she was overwhelmed by the distinctive odor of cat urine. There were seemingly hundreds of feral cats that had moved in and had not only made themselves at home but had destroyed the upholstered furniture and our bedding. Only a real friend would have gone through what she did to send us all the things worth saving. We put everything into storage for the day when we could afford an apartment.

I was feeling strangely ungainly and weird things were happening to my body, so I went to a doctor recommended by the agent's wife only to find out that I was pregnant! I rushed home to Villa Elaine to find Theo shaving in the small bathroom.

"Guess what," I cooed. "I'm pregnant!"

He just looked in the mirror and muttered, "Oh no!"

Well, gee whiz. I was devastated. I walked back into our living/bedroom and burst into tears. He, finally realizing I was there, rushed out, pulled me into his arms and reassured me that he was indeed thrilled, how wonderful, etc. etc. We even went out to a restaurant to celebrate, but I still thought the Oh No was the true thing he was feeling....no job...what was he going to do?...how was he going to provide? I understood the frustration but knew better days were on the horizon. Soon, just as I had predicted, he got his first job. We were ecstatic and then when the second came, we began looking for an apartment where we could bring up a child.

We found a lovely one-bedroom apartment on Chandler Boulevard in the Valley. It was walking distance to a small village with a market, post office and several shops. Our furniture was taken out of storage and in we moved.

I was a very happy child bearer. I loved all the attention I was getting from the yentas in the building and hubby was as solicitous and loving as he could be. I had made several friends by this time, wives of actors he had known in New York and who were also trying to get work in Los Angeles. One had two children, and another was pregnant at the same time as I, so I had lots of advice, wanted and unwanted, mostly about the birth process, which I really didn't want to hear. I was going to have a painless, quick birth and that was that.

THE OSCARS
1960

Through Theo's agent, we were invited to the Motion Picture Arts and Sciences Governors Ball at the Beverly Hilton Hotel which was held after the Academy Award ceremonies were over at The Pantages Theatre. It was April 4, 1960 and I was hugely pregnant. Theo gave me carte blanche to buy something appropriate for the occasion, and I found a beautiful navy silk dress that was perfect. Unlike today, it was unheard of to show one's belly. It just wasn't done. There were shops that specialized in cover up garments and there were whole sections of department stores that sold muumuus and caftans that looked like tents.

What an amazing evening. Everyone who was anyone, except us, were there. The stars were really stars then. They glittered, glowed and gleamed in their mysterious ways. Never before had I experience such glamour...these creatures were behaving like ordinary people, eating the same food, dancing on the same floor and there I was mingling with so many of my favorites over the years. There were Paul Newman and Joanne Woodward, Rock Hudson, who was forced by the studio to keep his sexual preference secret until the dreaded HIV, that took so many of the boys, revealed it. Shelley Winters who won Best Supporting Actress for *The Diary of Anne Frank*, Kirk Douglas bigger than life, Doris Day more beautiful in person and John Wayne looking elegant in his tux.

The first table going to and from the dance floor was occupied by none other than Ginger Rogers! She smiled and waved, like the Queen, and all stopped to pay their respects and give kisses on each cheek. As we were dancing, Elizabeth Taylor swirled my way giving me an extremely close-up view of her truly purple eyes. On the rebound from the terrible death of Mike Todd, her escort for the evening was her new husband, Eddie Fisher, who would, after a tantalizing scandal, soon be left for the magnetic Richard Burton. Tony Curtis and Janet Leigh were there, beautiful with the perfect marriage. But even movie stars have marital problems and their differences would soon put an end to the perfection. I encouraged Theo to really throw me around when we were jitterbugging as I thought it would be wonderful for his career if I were to give birth right there on the dance floor, but it was not to be for another month.

Some of the Oscar winners that year were Charlton Heston who won Best Actor for *Ben Hur*, over Jack Lemon, Jimmy Stewart, Lawrence Harvey and Paul Muni. I personally thought that any one of them were better actors than Heston and was heavily in favor of gorgeous Lawrence Harvey for *Room at the Top*, especially since Simone Signoret, his co-star, took home the Oscar for best actress. Ms. Signoret was soon to be embroiled in a scandal as her husband, the famous French singer/actor, Yves Montand began a torrid affair with Marilyn Monroe while they were filming *Let's Make Love*. The affair led to the breakup of Marilyn's and Arthur Miller's marriage, which according to the tabloids, was floundering

anyway, but the Montands, being French and having different views of infidelity, stayed married until Signoret's death
in 1985. *Ben Hur* won just about every category including Best
Picture. It was indeed an amazing, spectacular film, but I
didn't think it should have won over such rich dramas as
Anatomy of a Murder, The Diary of Anne Frank, The Nun's Story
or, *Room at the Top*. Juanita Moore, nominated for Best Supporting Actress for *Imitation of Life*, was only the third person
of color nominated in that category up to that time and not
that many since. In fact, since Hattie McDaniel won in that
category in 1939, it wasn't until 1963 that Sidney Poitier took
home an Oscar for Best Actor in *Lilies of the Field*. When the
wonderful evening was over, we went back to our apartment
and I fell into bed and dreamed of the stars and of the future
when my husband would receive an Oscar and we would be
glamorous and perfect.

AND BABY MAKES THREE
1960

My idea of a perfect and easy birth was not to be. The small hospital where my doctor practiced was overcrowded that evening and I was unceremoniously put in the hall on a gurney where I stayed until I was ready to enter the operating room. I'll just say it was a reeeeallllllly long time but with the help of drugs my darling baby girl was born at 2:40 P.M. on Thursday, May 5th, 1960.

We started the baby thing…up all night, exhausted etc. We developed a pattern, as most new parents do, of dividing the responsibility. Theo cleaned the bottles and gave her the middle of the night feeding so I could sleep, and I did the laundry and the taking care of her during the day. I had tried to breast-feed, but it was not a time when it was accepted and there was no one to help me. Actually, breast-feeding was viewed as disgusting and women who dared to feed their babies in public were vocally castigated.

I had gained an enormous amount of weight but with the help of the infamous Jack LaLanne and his TV workouts managed to get back to my old svelte self soon.

My mother and father came to help out soon after baby was born. They really were of tremendous help and even accepted Theo as their son-in-law. My father was particularly good with the baby and she gooed and gurgled every time he picked her up. It was really the best visit I could remember having with them. I guess having a grandchild just naturally invites love.

Theo was getting some work and some of the pressure was lifted off of him, so he was more present and willing to help. Suddenly, we were told we had to move, as there were no children allowed in the building. Well, they knew I was pregnant so why did they rent to us in the first place? Good question, no answer. We started looking again and finally found an apartment in West Hollywood. It was lovely, two bedrooms, new carpet and a small terrace. Heaven! We moved and life went on with the huge exception that work had dried up for Theo. He wasn't even getting any auditions. The angst was large and noisy. We began to have serious fights with me taking the brunt of his pain. I felt captured. Theo was terribly depressed and seldom got out of his pajamas or bothered to shave. He just sulked and fumed around the apartment all day, every day.

The baby was darling, funny and bright, but even she couldn't cheer him up or help fill the loss of identity I felt when being verbally assaulted and put down. Then, a miracle occurred. He was asked to be on a committee for Actor's Equity and thus began his lifelong involvement with first Equity and then later the Screen Actors Guild. He was needed again which helped restore his dignity and for me it was a Godsend to have him out of the house. He now had other people on whom to vent and when home he maintained a constant litany of injustices and downright treachery as perceived by him and his cronies that were practiced by the leaders of the union and the producers. I was bored by this talk but tried to listen patiently and utter the appropriate sounds of support when he stopped for a second or two.

We had parties in our small apartment with other actors and their wives, most of whom were transplants from Manhattan hoping to catch the gravy train when it stopped. Unfortunately, most ended up either going back to New York or struggling to get even small parts on television. Theo, with his Mediterranean looks and pock marked face had an advantage as he could play numerous roles. He could be a Middle Eastern potentate, or a mafia capo. When I was in my seventh month of pregnancy, Theo got a job in Italy in an episode of a series being shot there. I was distraught when the doctor said it wouldn't be wise to travel that distance as something might happen to the baby due to the pressure in the plane. I brooded over the fantasy that if I had just gone anyway everything would have been fine. The baby would have been born in Rome and Theo would have been a natural for the popular Spaghetti Westerns. I could study Italian and maybe be discovered myself!

Our life together was good when Theo was not depressed and ranting about one thing or another. The baby was a delight and smart and we both reveled in every new discovery she made. My relationship with my parents had never been better. Theo, the baby and I drove to Texas for Christmas and enjoyed the fuss made over her at all the friends' and family gatherings. All in all, it was a perfectly normal life, but I was miserable. In many ways I was still a child myself and completely unprepared emotionally to take on the responsibility of a husband and a baby. I think had I not gotten pregnant so soon after getting married, the adjustment to living with another complicated human being would have been easier. Then, when a baby came, I would have been ready. I just couldn't understand how my girlfriends seemed to be so happy to be wives and mothers. They gladly accepted the responsibility of wifedom and celebrated motherhood. I loved Theo and the baby, but it just wasn't enough. I was an open wound and more than eager and ready for anything or anyone whom I thought could heal me, make me whole again and take me away from reality. Hope appeared in the guise of an adoring young girl who did heal me for a while. Because of our relationship and the others I made during this relatively short period of my life, I believe I was able to finally heal myself. The trauma I endured during this time and the subsequent sacrifices I made for the sake of my child were my stepping-stones to maturity. It took a long time, but I finally discarded my Scarlett fantasy in order to become a mature and responsible woman. I have been able, through the rest of my long life, to take on the responsibility of caring for others with love and gratitude. I have to thank Mindy for that because without her I never would have learned who I was, what I was capable of or known that love is always a gift to be cherished and held tight.

THERE IS ALWAYS AN AFTERWARDS¶

There is always an afterwards, and mine has been as long and complicated, as life is.

Mindy? Well, I never saw her again, my loss, and I can only hope that she has had a good life filled with love and joy. After ten years, Theo and I divorced again. He met and married a lovely woman, with whom he found true love. My daughter grew up, has had a fulfilling career, and a truly gifted artist husband. I met and married yet another actor…sucker for punishment, but this time got it right. I stopped teaching to finally fulfil my dream of acting again. My husband and I had a wonderful and adventure-filled life together until his death in 2020, a really terrible year all around. I have been blessed with good health, still have all my marbles and most importantly, a keen sense of the absurd, or how else could I have survived all that I have.

And now, at eighty-six, look back on a life well-lived with, I hope, more to come. What more could any one person ask for?

I want to thank Tom Holbrook and Piscataqua Press. My husband Richard Herd who put up with me through endless rewrites. My first editor, Resa Alboher and Maryhop Brandon without whom none of this would have happened.